Breaking Up
&
Bouncing
Back

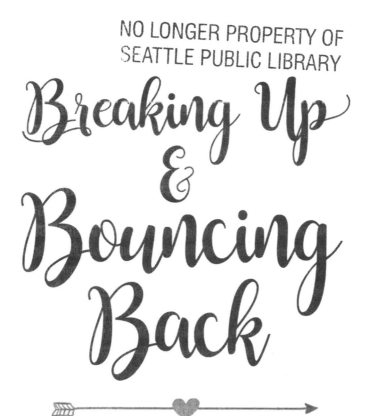

Breaking Up & Bouncing Back

Moving On to Create
the Love Life You Deserve

Samantha Burns LMHC
"The Millennial Love Expert"

ixia
PRESS

Mineola, New York

Bibliographical Note

Breaking Up & Bouncing Back: Moving On to Create the Love Life You Deserve is a new work, first published by Ixia Press in 2018.

Library of Congress Cataloging-in-Publication Data

Names: Burns, Samantha, author.
Title: Breaking up and bouncing back : moving on to create the love life you
   deserve / Samantha Burns.
Description: Mineola, New York : Ixia Press, 2018.
Identifiers: LCCN 2018003214| ISBN 9780486823959 | ISBN 0486823954
Subjects: LCSH: Separation (Psychology) | Man-woman relationships. |
   Interpersonal relations. | Dating (Social customs)
Classification: LCC BF575.G7 B86 2018 | DDC 646.7/7—dc23
LC record available at https://lccn.loc.gov/2018003214

Ixia Press
An imprint of Dover Publications, Inc.

Manufactured in the United States by LSC Communications
82395401   2018
www.doverpublications.com/ixiapress

For Darren, my ideal match.

For my parents, for providing unconditional love
and support.

For my best friends, who visited, called, and
gave me belonging when I felt lost.

For my heartbreak, without which I never would have
known how strong I am, or been challenged
to step up and create the love life I deserved.

CONTENTS

PREFACE: MY BIG BREAKUP ix

ACKNOWLEDGMENTS xv

INTRODUCTION xvii

SECTION 1: Surviving Your Breakup and Learning from
Your Love Lessons 1

Chapter 1: Emotional Roller Coaster 3

Chapter 2: Stages of Breakup Grief 8

Chapter 3: Self-Care Survival Skills 20

Chapter 4: Tough Love for a Tough Breakup 33

Chapter 5: Cold Turkey Cutoff vs. Hanging-on Hookup 43

Chapter 6: Get Out of My Head 61

Chapter 7: Understanding Your Breakup 75

Chapter 8: Reframe Your Breakup—
Pain into Wisdom Gained 90

Chapter 9: Status "Quoples" 111

SECTION 2: Cultivating Self-Love and Creating
New Purpose 117

Chapter 10: Self-Love Is the Best Love. 119

Chapter 11: Getting Back Out There. 126

Chapter 12: Here I Am 133

Chapter 13: Realistic Dating Mind-sets 140

SECTION 3: Life beyond Breakup 153

Chapter 14: Your Ideal Match 155

Chapter 15: Core Values and Relationship Requirements in
Intentional Dating 169

Chapter 16: Dating Questions Answered. 180

CONCLUSION. 213

BIBLIOGRAPHY 215

BOOKS TO ADD TO YOUR COLLECTION 221

ABOUT THE AUTHOR 222

My Big Breakup

I was in zombie mode. I sat propped up in bed, somewhere between dozing off and delusional. My body ached and for days I had no appetite. As I took shallow breaths, I felt like I was physically dying, but the only thing that was hurt was my heart. In fact, it was broken—shattered into a million pieces.

Four-and-a-half years of hope, commitment, love, effort, and financial investment squandered after the BS statement, "It's just not right." Excuse me? This was not the plan. We were supposed to be moving to California together, but I was resolved not to move across the country *again* without a ring on my finger. Yet, this was no surprise; we'd talked about the idea of getting engaged for well over a year. Memories raced through my mind: falling in love, transferring out of a doctoral program to be closer to him, moving from sunny Florida to blizzardy Boston, camping, hiking, vacations, silly Halloween costumes, cooking crepes, sticking by his side when he hated his job and was miserable, deceptive conversations about a future together. I felt rejected, abandoned, and completely alone.

The situation was so unfair. I had nothing to show for the effort I put into the relationship, besides a broken heart and shared furniture that I now needed to sell on Craigslist. I thought no one else in the world knew the pain I was going through. Typically strong, confident, and secure, I felt weak, rejected, and not good enough. While all my friends were progressing with their significant others, I was filled with dread and resentment that I had to start over. Woe is me, right? Yes, I recognized that it could be much worse, but in those dark days, I was stuck and in pain. Questions swirled through my mind, obsessing about why we broke up, how I could win him back, and why love wasn't enough. I had many nights of barely sleeping, I lost weight, it was difficult to function at work, and I randomly burst into tears multiple times a day. My shock, then denial, spiraled into devastation and depression. The intense anger came later.

We made the difficult decision to live together and remain in an emotional and physical relationship until he moved to California three months later. I know what you're thinking—yes, it was torture! But I wasn't ready to find a new apartment and move out knowing he still lived nearby. Our lives were tangled and enmeshed. Worst of all, in some twisted way, I thought maybe if I had three more months I could convince him he was making a terrible mistake. Maybe if I seduced him after work, baked lasagna, and went camping in the rain, somehow I'd be the perfect girlfriend and he'd realize that he couldn't live without me. Where was my awareness that if he didn't think I was The One after four years of dating, three months wouldn't make a difference? I was so blinded by love and fear of failure that I couldn't see reality.

He said he still loved me, but just didn't think it was "right." The best reason he could come up with was that I wasn't outdoorsy enough, despite my willing and positive participation in hiking and camping trips. Hell, I was the best s'mores roaster in all of New England! He couldn't clearly communicate why he ended the relationship, and I ruminated on his motivation for months, which made it harder to move on. I wanted an articulate and rational explanation. I deserved worthy reasons! I learned that love does not conquer all without both partners equally invested.

During our last three months together (I call this a *hanging-on hookup*, which you'll read about later), I was constantly stressed and sad. At one point, I printed out forty-four pictures of us from different events and dates and hung them up the entire staircase, hoping to tug on his heartstrings. I mailed a card to his office that listed the top ten outdoor activities to do in San Diego, saying, "I want to do these with you." Now, I cringe thinking about these desperate measures. Ultimately, you should not have to convince, beg, or threaten someone to be with you.

I relied heavily on my parents, calling them almost every day in tears. I called all of my closest friends, giving them the play-by-play and keeping them updated about the breakup and whether there was a chance of us getting back together. I hung onto every word, every detail that my ex provided. I found myself talking in circles, sharing the same thoughts and feelings over and over again. I exhausted myself, and worried that I exhausted my support network. At one point during a phone call with my mother, she yelled, "He doesn't love you anymore!" Ouch, right? I needed to hear it, but the pathetic thing was this only helped for a few minutes until I began ruminating again about why we couldn't make it work. I feared that I was becoming a burden to those closest to me, so I tried to keep it to myself as much as I could. The breakup had taken over my life and consumed me. I felt shame and embarrassment for not getting over it faster.

When my ex and I finally parted, I drove home to Pennsylvania to spend a long weekend with my parents. I needed the support, familiarity, and comfort that came with being at home. When I headed back to Boston, my brother came up to help me move. I also asked two of my closest friends to visit the first weekend I spent in my new apartment so that I wasn't alone. I think the best thing that happened to me was finding two women to live with in an awesome apartment just outside of downtown Boston in a popular area with tons to do. One housemate was single and we instantly became close friends, doing activities together and bonding over online dating adventures. The other housemate was active and outdoorsy, so she became my new hiking buddy.

I began exploring new hobbies and filling my social calendar, trying to stay as busy as possible. That doesn't mean it was smooth sailing. Did I spend nights crying myself to sleep and masochistically cyberstalking my ex on Facebook, quoting sappy song lyrics in hopes he'd read it and reach out? You bet I did. But, I eventually learned that I needed to set boundaries and cut off communication. Slowly, not overnight, I stopped thinking about my ex. It went from minute to minute of surviving, to multiple weeks strung together without allowing him to cross my mind. Within a few months, I began to feel optimistic about my independence, my newfound confidence, and the opportunity for a fresh start at love. I was rebuilding my life, figuring out what I wanted in an ideal partner, and trying to create closure from my breakup, all while online dating. Just three months after my heart was shattered, I went on a first date with a very special man who had husband-worthy qualities.

I wish I could say it was all kittens and rainbows moving forward, but we had a hiccup when my ex reached out six months after our breakup, saying he missed me, thought he made a mistake, and was questioning whether we should've gotten engaged. Do you know how many hours I wasted fantasizing about this exact scenario, and now it was actually happening? But so much had changed since he left, and I wanted more out of a relationship, like a reciprocal expression of intimacy and closeness, shared core values, and for him to better speak my love languages. I realized that in our old relationship I had compromised too much on some big-ticket items, which is something I would have never realized had I not gone through the breakup and gained valuable experience by dating different people.

After a few very difficult conversations with my ex, and a flight to California to talk in person, we agreed that it was really over. In fact, upon seeing me again he said he was hoping to feel differently, but now felt confident he made the right decision to end it. Stab me in the heart again, why don't you! However, by the time I landed back in Boston, I finally felt that I had enough closure to give my heart completely to someone else. This special someone even picked me up from the airport and shoveled my car out of the snow at 1:00 a.m. A few days later, the man who had patiently waited for me to be ready for an exclusive relationship became my boyfriend. Six months into dating we were in love, ten months in we moved in together, and on the one-year anniversary of our first date he popped the question—and we got married less than a year later! It was a whirlwind romance, but I'd never been more certain of a decision in my entire life—he was my person, and I would've never realized it if I hadn't gone through my heartbreak.

I became a true expert on myself, learning about what I needed and wanted out of a life partner, which I call *love lessons*. I engaged in valuable self-reflective work, learned about my attachment style, and drew conclusions about past emotional injuries, which inspired me to be a smarter, more intentional dater who avoided repeating negative patterns. I committed to loving myself and putting my needs first. I redefined my self-concept, increased self-esteem, and gave myself a more methodical approach to dating. I will help you do the same. Within one year of my breakup, my life looked completely different and better than I could've ever imagined. I successfully gained closure; I blasted through fitness goals and made new friendships; I quit my agency job; I founded my own clinical counseling practice; I launched LoveSuccessfully.com, my virtual coaching business; I started writing this book; and, most important, I got engaged to the love of my life!

Breakups aren't trivial; they affect us at our core. My own heartbreak motivated me to do research in order to learn as much as possible about the breakup process, from both an emotional and physical/neurochemical standpoint, so that I could bring this specialized knowledge into my work as a licensed mental health counselor and later as a dating coach. My personal experience allows me to connect more deeply and authentically in my work helping clients bounce back from soul-crushing splits to create love lives that thrive. It's allowed me to be more direct, compassionate, and empathetic, which I hope shines through as you work your way through this book. My goal in writing *Breaking Up & Bouncing Back* is to normalize this breakup experience for you, make you feel validated and understood, and, most important, for you to know that you're not alone. It takes so much courage to be vulnerable, to sit with the pain that you're experiencing right now, and to take action to get the support you need. Unfortunately, I cannot hit fast-forward so that you can skip over this breakup—believe me, my dear, I wish I could. Instead, I can provide you with the support and foundational skills you need to survive, move on, and find a more ideal match. Though every relationship and heartbreak is unique, there is a formula to treating this universal experience and bouncing back successfully. You'll learn these key coping skills and techniques throughout the chapters, so that once you reach the end, your heart will be healed and your love life will be ready to blossom.

ACKNOWLEDGMENTS

Thank you to my all-star agent, Jennifer Chen Tran, who found me on Instagram and believed in me and this book from the moment she started reading my posts about healing, dating, and the love we all deserve. As a first-time author, I appreciate you for teaching me about the process, for cheering me on and supporting me in this long and exciting journey! I am so grateful for my editor, Nora Rawn, who resonated with the content of this book and believed in my vision that no one should have to go through heartbreak alone. Thank you to my publisher, Jennifer Feldman, and to the dedicated staff at Ixia Press and Dover Publications for publishing this book and bringing this wholehearted project to life!

INTRODUCTION

Congratulations! Why am I congratulating you? It's not because you've hit the bottom of the Chunky Monkey ice cream container, it's because you're actively taking steps to work through your breakup. And you want to hear something glorious? There's life after a breakup. Every setback is a setup for a comeback, and yours will be fierce. If you're wallowing in the depths of your heartbreak, then you probably want to throw this book at me right now, but I promise it's true. There's life after a painful, soul-crushing, shameful, feels-like-you-lost-the-love-of-your-life-and-can-barely-breathe breakup. I'm living proof.

Say goodbye to zombie mode. It's time to begin your transformative journey to a healed heart and more fulfilling love life. Think of this book as your road map to breaking up and bouncing back. Your world may have come crashing down, but there's secure, healthy, and happy love out there. But first we have to get your breakup grief in check, reflect on your love lessons, identify negative patterns, rebuild and release your inner confidence, get laser-focused on what you need in a partner, and learn how to analyze your dating data so that you can become a smarter, more intentional dater. If you're sarcastically thinking, "*Pff*, that's *all*?" don't feel overwhelmed; I've got you, girl! I'll be here walking you through every step of the way.

What would normally take months of expensive therapy, I'll deliver to you short and sweet in this book. As a licensed mental health counselor and dating coach specializing in relationship issues and healing broken hearts, I'm putting my best stuff right here in your hands. Throughout the book, I've referred to my own personal experiences, as well as those of my clients, whose confidentiality I've protected by changing identifying information. Through my research and work, I'm always blown away that despite our differences in individual stories, much of our emotional and neurochemical experiences during heartbreak and falling in love are quite similar. So whether you were cheated on, were ghosted, didn't feel like a priority, couldn't communicate and repair conflicts, had different emotional needs, argued over sex or money, didn't feel safe and secure in the relationship, weren't on the same page about what you wanted in life, or fell out of love, this book is for you.

Beside your box of tissues, you'll create your own Bounce Back Journal, in which you'll respond in depth to the exercises throughout the book. As a therapist, it's my job to ask challenging questions that increase insight into your thoughts and behaviors. The awareness you gain from these exercises will be extremely valuable in your bounce-back journey. Plus, writing is a beneficial tool to aid in identifying and gaining control of your emotions. It's a quiet time to transfer all of those swirling thoughts from your mind concretely onto paper, which can be quite healing in itself.

Before we get started, just a heads-up that throughout the book I use the term "breakup," but it's appropriate for someone going through a divorce too. I also write mostly about straight couples, but my advice generally holds true for individuals of any sexual orientation or gender, and I've opted to use the singular pronoun "they" to be as inclusive as possible. So without further ado, let's kick this off and begin your transition from heartbroken to wholehearted!

SECTION 1

Surviving Your Breakup and Learning from Your Love Lessons

*I think that little by little
I'll be able to solve my
problems and survive.*

FRIDA KAHLO

CHAPTER 1

Emotional Roller Coaster

Forget period cramps, bad hair days, hangovers, breakouts, getting fired, the guilt you feel after you've eaten a half-dozen donuts by yourself, or even a fight with a dear friend—few things feel worse than the way you are likely feeling right now. Newly single has left you dazed, confused, and feeling as though you've been stabbed in the heart. You feel like your entire world collapsed, like your body may explode, and you're numb from crying so much.

No matter your role in this breakup, whether you were dumped or you walked away, it takes serious courage and resiliency to make it through to the other side. Your whole life is changing, and the unknown can be scary. You suddenly shifted from a "we" to a "me," no longer having to consider someone else in your plans and daily routine. Flying solo and making decisions as an individual can be overwhelming. You've learned to rely on someone else for emotional support, and to share living responsibilities.

It's hard to be optimistic about a happy future love life when you're dealing with the painful nuisances of getting back all of your stuff, finding a new place to live, and running into him and his new girlfriend at your old favorite coffee shop—you still can't believe he had the indecency to bring her there! You may be wallowing in self-pity, questioning if you're doomed to be alone forever. You're consumed by thoughts of the breakup, and nothing seems to distract you. Your mind is racing and only one person is running through your mind—your ex.

So why do you care so much about this breakup? Why is it so challenging to stand up and be strong on your own? The answer is because at our core, we are a species that survives and thrives on giving and receiving love. We are animals who spend the longest time being reared by our parents, depending on someone to care for us from infancy through our teen years. We regulate our emotions through our connections. Studies with both monkeys and human orphans have shown that growing up in isolation without physical comfort and love is likely to produce adults with disturbed cognitive and emotional behavior, and early death. We have evolved to be in close, intimate relationships—it's our primal need, so much so that our brain chemistry and nervous systems are affected by those closest to us. Rejection is one of the most excruciating human experiences because it makes us feel alone, unvalued, unprotected, and that we don't matter. We feel like we've been left for dead, and that we can no longer depend on the person we trusted most. "Can I rely on you to be there for me? When I turn to you, can I depend on you to respond to my needs? Do you value, respect, and accept me? Do I matter to you? Do you need me too?" Because you're going through a breakup, the answer to all of these questions is ultimately no, your partner is not there for you in the way that you need. This devastating realization can make you feel utterly alone and question if you will ever be able to trust and depend on a romantic partner again. In the aftermath of a breakup, you're missing your emotional home, your sense of connection and belonging in this world. The home that was supposed to protect your heart and keep you safe is the one that hurt you.

Science has shown that couples in happy and stable long-term relationships are better prepared to thrive. These couples are healthier: they have lower blood pressure, decreased stress, anxiety, physical pain, and they live longer. When in a loving relationship, individuals view themselves more positively, they're more confident in solving problems, and they are more likely to achieve their individual goals. So when we are rejected, our world comes crashing down and we're at greater risk physically and emotionally. On a biological basis, your breakup is processed as a survival threat and is a huge trauma to your life.

Right now your heartbreak probably has you questioning the very concept of love, lacking a sense of belonging, and writhing with a deep sense of shame. Researcher and author Brené Brown captures the interdependent relationship between love, shame, and belonging in *The Gifts of Imperfection*, in which she defines these concepts as follows:

> *Love:* We cultivate love when we allow our most vulnerable and powerful selves to be deeply seen and known . . . Love is not something we give or get; it is something that we nurture and grow, a connection that can only be cultivated between two people when it exists within each one of them—we can only love others as much as we love ourselves . . . Shame, blame, disrespect, betrayal, and the withholding of affection damage the roots from which love grows.

> *Belonging:* The innate human desire to be part of something larger than us . . . We often try to acquire it by fitting in and by seeking approval, which are not only hollow substitutes for belonging, but often barriers to it. Because true belonging only happens when we present our authentic, imperfect selves to the world, our sense of belonging can never be greater than our level of self-acceptance.

> *Shame:* The intensely painful feeling or experience of believing that we are flawed and therefore unworthy of love and belonging.

Keep these definitions in mind, as we'll work on increasing self-love, decreasing shame, and opening yourself to vulnerability along the way in your bounce-back journey.

WHAT SHOULD YOU EXPECT TO FEEL DURING YOUR BREAKUP?

Though the content and context of everyone's breakup may be unique, there are common emotional experiences and stages of grief that we tend to go through. Do any of these feel familiar?

- ♥ Ruminative
- ♥ Despondent
- ♥ Numb
- ♥ Enraged
- ♥ Betrayed
- ♥ Blindsided

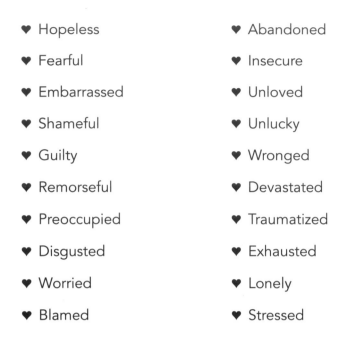

- ♥ Hopeless
- ♥ Fearful
- ♥ Embarrassed
- ♥ Shameful
- ♥ Guilty
- ♥ Remorseful
- ♥ Preoccupied
- ♥ Disgusted
- ♥ Worried
- ♥ Blamed

- ♥ Abandoned
- ♥ Insecure
- ♥ Unloved
- ♥ Unlucky
- ♥ Wronged
- ♥ Devastated
- ♥ Traumatized
- ♥ Exhausted
- ♥ Lonely
- ♥ Stressed

It wouldn't surprise me if you nodded along to every single adjective. Many of the words listed above may be symptomatic of depression and anxiety, which are very real mental health disorders that should be treated by a professional. Symptoms of depression include feeling very sad, empty, or hopeless; tearfulness; losing interest or pleasure in most activities; loss of appetite or emotional eating that result in changes in weight; insomnia or hypersomnia; low energy; fatigue; feelings of worthlessness or excessive guilt; difficulty concentrating; and, in severe cases, thoughts of suicide. Symptoms of anxiety include worry, feeling on edge, jitteriness, nervousness, difficulty concentrating, irritability, muscle tension, and sleep disturbance. People going through a breakup are often told to get over it, or are left to fend for themselves, and the pain of their breakup goes untreated or even unacknowledged. But a breakup can be a monumental moment in your life, changing the course of your life forever.

I don't want to minimize or diminish what you may be feeling right now. We're so used to intellectualizing our feelings and not being tuned into our bodies that it's challenging to connect to yourself on an emotional level. You're likely experiencing numerous, conflicting emotions at once, and it's important to take the time now to identify them. Research actually shows that when you become mindfully aware of your emotions and label them, they won't feel as strong. It sounds too simple to be true, but it works. That's because when you think about what feelings you are experiencing, this mental effort activates the right ventrolateral prefrontal cortex, a brain region responsible for emotional regulation. We know through science that when you don't take time to identify your emotions there's no decreased response in the brain region called the amygdala, which helps process feelings, and your emotions can actually be more intense and harder to understand. Once you label the emotions, you don't need to do anything radical or rash to numb or change them; just observe them gently and kindly without judgment. Know that you're able to experience these emotions, and despite their feeling intense, they are not static or permanent. The rest of you can hold strong and watch these emotions roll in and out, like waves, coming and going. Imagine yourself flowing with them, instead of fighting against them, honoring each without resistance. This is your first step to healing.

Complete the following exercise, which will help you process and hold space for these intense emotions.

EXERCISE: PROCESSING YOUR EMOTIONS

Begin a daily exercise in your Bounce Back Journal with the following prompt:

- ♥ Today I'm feeling:
- ♥ On a scale from 1 to 10 (10 = most intense), I would rate this feeling as a:
- ♥ I noticed this feeling when _____
- ♥ Time of day I was feeling this way _____
- ♥ Length of time the emotion lingered _____

Create a separate entry for each notable emotion. Keep an eye out for any patterns, such as things that triggered your emotions or time of day you struggle the most. Notice that when you take the space to honor these feelings, each will start to become smaller and easier than the last, and the interval between them may lengthen, leaving you with more time to relax, be still, and be at peace.

CHAPTER 2

Stages of Breakup Grief

Going through a breakup is actually very similar to grieving a death. You're grieving the loss of someone you love and learning to live life without them by your side. You may have heard that there are five stages of grief, originally identified by Elisabeth Kübler-Ross, which can also be applied to a breakup. The five stages of breakup grief are *denial, bargaining, anger, depression*, and *acceptance*. It's like a roller-coaster ride with a long and twisted track. Your emotions are so mixed up that you bounce around from one extreme to another on a daily basis. Though it may not feel like it right now, eventually you'll come full circle and the track will straighten for a safe landing. In fact, a yearlong German study found that for teens and young adults dealing with a breakup, their self-esteem rebounded by the following year, even if they remained single. There are no rules as to how long you'll spend in each stage of breakup grief. Some days you'll feel like you touched on all of them. Some weeks you'll question, "When will I just get through this?" It takes time and active effort, and is most helpful when you are kind and compassionate with yourself, instead of judgmental and self-critical.

Don't compare your own breakup recovery to the pace at which you *think* your ex is moving on. I know you want to hear that they're just as devastated as you are because in some way this will validate the importance

People are like stained glass windows. They sparkle and shine when the sun is out, but when the darkness sets in their true beauty is revealed only if there is light from within.

ELISABETH KÜBLER-ROSS

of the relationship, but people process and cope in different ways and at different speeds. Rather than turn to your ex to hear that the relationship was meaningful or significant, tell yourself your own feelings are just as valid.

The stages of grief don't work in a linear fashion—you can jump from one stage to the next and revert back to more intense emotions at any point. One day you may feel like you've finally reached acceptance, and then you walk past the restaurant where you had your first date and all of a sudden you're sad or angry again. This typically happens when you've been exposed to a trigger. When I say trigger, I mean something or someone that reminds you of your ex and elicits powerful emotions and memories. Triggers can pop up out of the blue and be difficult to anticipate, and often lead to intrusive thoughts. If you experienced any trauma in the relationship, such as physical or emotional abuse, you might experience things like flashbacks and physical symptoms, such as shaking, muscle tension, and shortness of breath, after encountering a trigger. The good news is that with time you begin to bounce back from these intense emotions more quickly. Here's a breakdown of the emotional stages of a breakup and some tips on surviving them:

DENIAL

In this stage, it hasn't sunk in that the relationship is over. We can't believe this is the end. We cling to hope that it will work out and we can't accept our new reality. We may feel disbelief and totally paralyzed. Sometimes we can feel physically and emotionally numb.

In this stage, you may wake up and for a blissful moment think that you are still together. You hope they'll realize they made a mistake and come back to you. You might even be that person who refuses to accept that you've split up, so you text or engage with them on social media as if nothing has happened.

SURVIVING DENIAL

You can breathe a sigh of relief that denial is normal. Anytime you're faced with a big transition or trauma, denial and shock allow you to adjust to what happened as you begin to comprehend all the ways in which your life is about to change. It's kind of like survival mode for your mind. To help reality set in, talk with trusted friends and supportive family members. It may take one of them shouting like my mom did, "He doesn't love you anymore," for it to sink in, if only for a moment.

One of the things that may shift you out of denial is changing your daily routine. You and your ex likely shared many rituals and traditions, such as calling each other on your drive home from work or getting brunch together every Sunday. This is the time to start replacing those routine activities that you normally relied on with something else, like calling your best friend to chat about your day, or making sure you're busy with plans during particularly lonely parts of your week. One of the worst things or times for me was crawling into an empty bed at night, so I distracted myself with good books, podcasts, and music. You can also a put an essential oil diffuser next to your pillow, filling the room with scents for relaxation, stress, and sleep. If you're stuck in denial, my tough love discussion in chapter 4 may be exactly what you need to hear.

BARGAINING/ANXIETY

I've added the word "anxiety" to go along with the bargaining stage because it's a prevalent emotion that many people feel when experiencing significant loss and going through a major life transition. In this stage we try our best to win our ex back and make the relationship work. We may beg, demand, negotiate, and make unrealistic promises. We try to shift our lives around to give the relationship another chance. We have tunnel vision that the only way to be happy again is to get back together. We worry about what life could look like without this person, and are overwhelmed with fear.

In this stage, you may promise your ex that you'll change or go to therapy. You might try calling your ex's friends to get them on your side and persuade them to help get the two of you back together. You tell your ex you can't live without them. Maybe you send their favorite cookies in the false hope that they can't live without them and you too. In my breakup story, remember how I hung all those pictures up on the wall and mailed him a card about the fun things we could do in San Diego? Yup, that was bargaining.

SURVIVING BARGAINING/ANXIETY

Ask yourself this: Are you trying to save the relationship because it's perfect and you love everything about your ex and the way they treat you; or, deep down, are you really afraid of change, starting over, or what other people will think about it not working out? If the relationship really was *so* perfect, would there have been a breakup in the first place?

Bargaining is a no-man's land where you're not making any progress. The more you talk, beg, and plead with your ex to be with you, the more stuck you become in believing that the only way to live life is with them. This is when the anxiety kicks in: fear about the future can be paralyzing, so you fight for the relationship instead of embracing change. The most important thing to tell yourself is that you should never have to convince someone to love you or want to be with you. During the relationship or breakup you may have received criticism or constructive feedback (that's for you to define) from your ex about your personality or behaviors. During this stage, you may realize there are things you want to work on about yourself. If you decide to change yourself, it needs to be because you value these changes and not as a ploy to win back your ex. There are many paths in life, so it's time to be flexible and resilient and begin your walk down another one.

ANGER

In this stage, we're furious at what happened. We're pissed things didn't go our way. Our anger can be directed at many people and things. For example, we can be angry at our ex for leaving and hurting us, angry at people who don't acknowledge our pain, angry at the other woman (if there is one), angry that the relationship went a different direction than we expected, angry at God and the universe, and angry at ourselves for putting up with less than we deserved or for investing so much love, energy, time, commitment, and finances into someone who hurt us. Anger is the body's physiological response to a perceived threat, which doesn't need to be tangible—it can be a perceived threat to a part of our identity or to our emotional safety. We are in a fight-or-flight mode and our body is in an arousal state flooded with the stress hormones cortisol and adrenaline, which rev us up.

In this stage, you may send nasty emails to your ex, trash-talk them to your friends, blast them on social media, throw away their belongings, or create conniving plans to embarrass them or get revenge. You may even frighten yourself by fantasizing about the ways in which you can hurt your ex's possessions, like keying their car. One of my male clients told me his ex-wife poured bleach on his suits while holding their infant! Thinking these vengeful thoughts and acting on them are very different, but in both cases you may not recognize yourself.

SURVIVING ANGER

To cope with anger, try to view the relationship in its totality and not allow all that was good to be lost in the bitterness of the breakup. Oftentimes people want to paint their ex as either pure evil or a total saint, but black-and-white thinking could cause more harm than good in the long term. Although anger can protect you temporarily, it can also prevent you from dealing with underlying feelings. I like to think of anger as a secondary emotion, so you need to explore beneath it. For instance, if you can instead be vulnerable to the underlying hurt and pain that anger often masks, then you can engage in a powerful healing experience in which you learn about yourself and identify your love lessons—the nuggets of wisdom that allow you to move forward and find a better match. When you feel lost in the white-hot anger, daydreaming of revenge, ask yourself, "How can I be more vulnerable in this moment?" If you asked your anger to step aside, what emotions would step in to replace it? You can allow the anger to linger, or you can use it as motivation to inspire positive change.

Friendships can be an invaluable resource in helping you work through anger. You can ask your besties to share the ways in which they didn't think you were your best self in the relationship, which is not the same as unproductive ex-bashing. Sometimes hearing an objective perspective can help you grasp how the relationship wasn't serving you and can shed some light onto how you may have given away your power or not valued yourself in the relationship. Tell your friends that you need them to be supportive in the coming days and weeks. Warn them in advance that if you're still fuming in a month or two and all of your conversations resort to trash-talking or taking the victim role, then they need to gently (or bluntly) call you out and give you that extra push to move forward in your grieving process.

One of the best ways to manage your anger is exercising, which is the perfect way to blow off rage and resentment. Whether you like to dance it out, run it out, or—my personal favorite—kick and punch it out, get your body moving. Anger is like an energetic upwelling in your body that needs a physical release. Now is the time to be adventurous and bravely sign up for a new workout routine. CrossFit, Zumba, Pilates, yoga, running clubs, stand-up paddle boarding, boot camps, rock climbing—your options are endless. Your mind and body will thank you, and a hot postbreakup bod doesn't hurt either! Plus, once you're in a better state of mind, the gym or your fitness community of choice is a great place to meet a health-conscious and motivated man.

DEPRESSION

In this stage, the overwhelming emotion is sadness. We may notice physical symptoms, like having low energy or feeling exhausted all of the time. We experience changes in eating and sleeping habits. We tend to isolate ourselves and lose motivation to do activities we normally enjoy. We may feel hopeless about the situation and about our futures. In severe cases, we may even have scary thoughts that life is not worth living, and a desire to hurt our ex or ourselves. When our partner exits our life, our attachment bond is broken, causing depression. Our internal systems actually synchronize with our partner's, which is called limbic resonance; this stimulates the release of certain neurochemicals that affect our emotional health and physical well-being. You see, our brains have evolved to share deep emotional states like empathy and fear, meaning our brain chemistry and nervous systems are affected by the people we're closest to. This intricate connection to our partners helps us to thrive, yet when the limbic resonance is severed and we lose our partner, depression ensues and we have to readjust.

A good indicator that you're in the depression stage is that you haven't washed your hair in days, or really done much of anything. You may have difficulty getting out of bed; you feel lethargic, mentally foggy, and irritable. Maybe you cancel plans with friends and family, or blow off a class to stay home alone and watch sappy movies and cry yourself to sleep. You may feel like nothing will ever get better. In this dark time, you might take the victim role, questioning your worthiness and reminding yourself of past hurts and how others have let you down, validating the messages you've internalized over the years about giving and receiving love and about belonging.

SURVIVING DEPRESSION

Although it's uncomfortable to feel depressed and dejected, you need to give yourself time and permission to experience these feelings, without acting impulsively to numb, self-medicate, or run away from them. I'll review some therapeutic exercises you can use to manage your depression and anxiety in chapter 6. If you notice that you're consistently missing work or school, isolating yourself, and having hopeless thoughts about life, you should seek support from a mental health professional. Call the suicide hotline or take yourself to the emergency room ASAP if you're thinking that life is not worth living and contemplating a plan to act on these thoughts.

I know being active sounds like the last thing you want to do when you have low energy and lack of motivation, but science proves exercise is a natural remedy for depression. Exercise releases endorphins and chemicals such as dopamine, which makes you feel pleasure and boosts your mood. It's an effective stress buster and helps manage anxiety and sleep. If you can't seem to get out of your own way, aim for a daily walk, and build from there.

ACCEPTANCE

In this stage, although it may not have been the outcome we initially wanted, we have learned to accept the breakup. We have made peace with the loss of our ex. We have gained emotional distance from the end of the relationship. This stage happens gradually over time.

By the time we reach acceptance, you have let go of the intense anger and sadness. There may be moments of hurt and loneliness, but your general attitude shifts toward optimism about the future. Though it was once unimaginable and full of pain, you can now see the upside to your new reality. You've had an awakening and are living a purposeful life. I remember waking up one morning, months after my big breakup, realizing that I hadn't cried or felt angry in a while; I felt lighter from letting these somber emotions go. At first it was a "one-day-at-a-time" approach, which over time strung together into multiple weeks, and eventually months. This mental freedom feels *ahhh*-mazing.

SURVIVING ACCEPTANCE

Think of acceptance as your long-term goal. I know I said there is no set timeline for each of these stages, but I can guarantee that after a big breakup no one reaches acceptance overnight or a week later. If you do, you're probably just back in denial. Initially, you'll obsess about the breakup, and it will feel like you can't get it off your mind. But, as you get closer to acceptance, you'll dwell on it less frequently, and you can go days and even weeks without thinking of "He Who Must Not Be Named."

From the initial shock to your current mood, whether it's regret, melancholy, or even hopefulness, it's very important to give yourself permission to think about and talk about the breakup. Research shows that people who process their breakups actually recover more quickly than those who compartmentalize everything. This can be done in different ways, such as talking to family and friends, writing in your Bounce Back Journal, meditating, or going to counseling. It's really about giving yourself time and space to mentally process the relationship, and *reframing* your experiences for a sense of control, power, and increased insight. Your realizations in this stage are essential in moving forward. These love lessons can be used in personal growth, like dating from a more authentic position, and creating a more congruent relationship that aligns with your desires. Acceptance is about letting go of who you were in the last relationship, embracing who you are now, and living more authentically to create the love life you desire in the future.

I also want to bring up the word *forgiveness*, which sometimes gets used synonymously with acceptance. Forgiveness does not happen all at once, and it doesn't mean you have to forget about what happened to you. It doesn't mean pardoning your ex's cruel or inappropriate behavior, nor does it make you weak or mean your own feelings are unjustified. Instead, forgiveness can be a way of healing yourself and moving on. It's a conscious act of releasing your ex from bitterness or disappointment and reclaiming this energy to move forward in your own love life. Lily Tomlin says, "Forgiveness means giving up all hope for a better past." When we forgive, we create mental space to stop judging and stop feeling guilty.

We like to torture ourselves, prolong misery and pain, and wallow in shame and self-loathing. We relive the gut-wrenching moments over and over—what they said when they dumped you, catching them with another woman (if there was one), the blowout arguments you had throughout the relationship. We waste precious emotional energy fueling negative feelings that keep you a prisoner of your own pain.

In *You Are a Badass: How to Stop Doubting Your Greatness and Start Living an Awesome Life*, author Jen Sincero writes, "Holding on to resentment is like taking poison and waiting for your enemies to die." You may never get that apology from your ex, but forgiveness can set you free mentally and emotionally. Sincero says, "The longer you stay attached to being vindicated, the longer they hang around in your consciousness, stinking up your life. Do not fall prey to the false belief that by forgiving someone you're letting them off the hook. Because when you forgive someone you let yourself off the hook. Forgiving them isn't about being nice to them, it's about being nice to yourself."

Though forgiving your ex, especially for egregious behavior, is not mandatory, I do believe *self-forgiveness* is required to move forward. And through the process of self-forgiveness, you may create space or willingness to forgive your ex too. Be aware that what you've judged in your ex, you've also judged in yourself. We project problems, qualities, and criticisms onto others that we fear or want ourselves. In the acceptance stage, you've forgiven yourself for losing your sense of self, for not liking or loving yourself, for not honoring your values, for compromising too much, for giving away your power, for being overly naïve or trusting, for ignoring your inner voice or suspicions, for lying to yourself, for your role in the relationship dissatisfaction, for tolerating excuses, for blaming yourself, for replaying and validating past emotional injuries, and for feeling as though you're not enough. Forgiveness is a conscious choice, and requires you to have compassion for yourself, and to love the parts of yourself that feel shameful. When I talk about forgiving your ex, sometimes all this means is seeing these human qualities in them too, and mentally sending loving vibes to their hurt and broken parts. You can shift out of toxic anger when you believe that if they caused you pain, they must have pain inside; wishing them the healing they need from afar. You release ill will when you embrace love for yourself and others. This doesn't need to be done in person, or even through conversation. Sometimes all it takes to cut the negative emotional cord is to send positive thoughts through prayer or meditation. Just be cautious of trying to grant forgiveness to your ex or to yourself before you're emotionally ready, in an attempt to relieve yourself from guilt or sadness. Forgiving your ex doesn't need to be a primary goal, but self-forgiveness, which we'll practice later in this book, can create closure and free you from harboring resentment, which eats away at you. You're not on a timeline for forgiveness; if you create space for it, it will come to you.

Now that you know about the stages of breakup grief, hopefully these emotions won't blindside you. No matter how much you read or prepare yourself, heartbreak is painful. Cut yourself some slack. Cry a little, or cry a lot. Remember, if you try to compartmentalize the pain too much, you're likely in denial and it will come back to bite you in the butt later on. Don't forget that you may cycle through and bounce around the stages multiple times before acceptance sticks. Part of being proactive in healing is also being patient with yourself. Don't put too much pressure on yourself to rush through each stage, and remember that you can't control time.

EXERCISE: WHICH STAGE AM I IN?

In your Bounce Back Journal create five sections, each labeled with a stage of grief (denial, bargaining/anxiety, anger, depression, and acceptance). As you go through the weeks and months postbreakup, use this space to write emotions, incidents, and experiences that fit into each category. Then, after each experience, identify one concrete thing you can do to survive this stage that will move you toward acceptance. For example:

Denial
July 28: I noticed myself fantasizing that my ex would reach out because we were supposed to go to his friend's wedding today. I thought maybe there was a small chance he'd call and ask me to still go with him.

Step I can take to move out of denial: Get dressed up anyway and make special plans with a friend so that I'm not sitting around wishing I was at that wedding with my ex.

Bargaining/Anxiety
August 5: Today I caved and texted him, "I've been thinking about you so much and still think you're making a huge mistake. Can we talk?"

Step I can take to move out of bargaining/anxiety: Acknowledge that I'm feeling really nervous and afraid of being alone right now, and remind myself that it's okay to feel this way and it doesn't mean he was perfect for me.

Anger

September 13: I can't believe he had the nerve to ask me to split the cost of breaking our lease. He should pay since he's the one who ended our relationship!

Step I can take to move out of anger: After work head straight to boxing class where I'll pretend I'm punching him in the face.

Depression

October 9: Today I heard he went on a date and I'm devastated that he's already moving on. How can he forget about me this fast?

Step I can take to move out of depression: I'll call my BFF Devan, she always knows exactly what to say to make me feel better.

Acceptance

November 20: Today I realized I'm actually feeling excited for Thanksgiving, whereas last month I was so sad about buying my flight home and that he wouldn't be coming with me.

Step I can take to stay in acceptance: Talk to my family about how I'm feeling and tell them I appreciate their support while I'm home celebrating the holiday.

Realize that inside of you, you have the vulnerability to let it hurt, the courage to let it heal, and the strength to let it go.

CHAPTER 3

Self-Care
Survival Skills

Somewhere along the way we prioritized pleasing our ex and put the relationship over our own personal needs. Now is the time for self-care. Self-care requires recognizing and prioritizing your own needs, creating balance in your life, and optimizing health and wellness. Self-care not only prepares you to take care of yourself, but impacts who you show up as in your relationships, and enables you to function better in both your personal and professional life. I first heard the term "self-care" in graduate school years ago, before it was buzzworthy. In some ways, I like to think of self-care as a less clinical term for coping skills, which are the many ways in which we can take care of ourselves physically, mentally, emotionally, and spiritually. Self-care needs to be be woven into our daily routines and treated as an important appointment with ourselves, or else it's easy to brush off. Self-care should be something that energizes us and recharges our battery, not something that drains us. In this day and age, there's so much emphasis on self-care that it may feel like one more thing to add to your ever-growing to-do list, which only makes you feel more stressed out, like when you blew off yoga class because something got in the way. Try to do small things and take actions that can be built realistically into your daily schedule, such as five minutes for meditation, taking a mindful walk rather than burying your head in your phone, refusing to check your work e-mails after 9:00 p.m., push-ups and sit-ups when you first

Rest and self-care are so important. When you take time to replenish your spirit, it allows you to serve others from the overflow. You cannot serve from an empty vessel.

ELEANOR BROWNN

wake up before the day gets away from you, a weekly lunch date with a friend, or making sure you have enough time to enjoy your cup of coffee while flipping through your favorite magazine. You define what feels good and rejuvenating for you, and keep in mind that some self-care is better than no self-care.

Surviving and thriving during difficult times comes down to caring for yourself, even when no one else does. Diane Von Furstenberg said it best: "The most important relationship in your life is the relationship you have with yourself. Because no matter what happens, you will always be with yourself."

SELF-CARE TOOL KIT

As soon as life gets rough, it's easy and usually unintentional to put your healthy habits on the back burner. But during this intense and transitional time, you need the stability that self-care routines provide.

Below are some self-care survival skills and activities to help you get through the most devastating breakup. When you can't seem to get out of zombie mode, turn to this list for inspiration:

- ♥ Exercise (bonus points if you try a new class or sign up for a 5K or Spartan race).

- ♥ Listen to music and create playlists that take you on an emotional journey you want to be on.

- ♥ Play with your pet (or borrow a friend's for an afternoon)— pets show us unconditional love.

- ♥ Deep-breathing exercises.

- ♥ Drink soothing herbal tea.

- ♥ Spend time in nature—take a walk in the woods, stroll on the beach, hike a mountain (studies found that time walking in nature can decrease the risk for depression).

- ♥ Volunteer—this isn't just about being a good citizen, research on volunteering has actually shown the act can increase social connection, ward off depression and loneliness, reduce stress, and increase a sense of life satisfaction.

- ♥ Dance around your house—just let loose, no one is watching!
- ♥ Watch cat videos on YouTube (or other videos that make you laugh out loud).
- ♥ Color. (I've bought an adult coloring book called *Have a Nice Life Asshole: Breakup Stress Reliever* for clients and friends, and they love it!)
- ♥ Light scented candles and watch a favorite movie.
- ♥ Give yourself a personal makeover (haircut and color, wardrobe, and new perfume since scent is closely linked with memory).
- ♥ Head to the library or bookstore and spend a couple of hours browsing topics that interest you.
- ♥ Lose yourself in a good novel.
- ♥ Actually use your vacation days—plan a trip with a friend or go on an adventure solo.
- ♥ Attend services at your religious institution of choice and utilize the power of prayer.

ADD YOUR OWN ♥

Self-care isn't just about emotions, either. When you don't take care of your body during a stressful time, you get sick, burn out, and suffer from irritability, low energy, and more serious mental health issues, such as anxiety and depression. The key to a balanced life is proper diet, sleep, and exercise. As soon as these three core self-care skills go out the window, your mood, energy, and motivation go with them. Your mental health is directly impacted by your physical health, so to survive this breakup, prioritize your mind and body and nurture your physiological needs.

DIET: EATING FOR YOUR BRAIN, BODY, AND BREAKUP

During difficult, chaotic, and sad times, we tend to overeat or undereat. The food-mood connection is real. Have you ever noticed that you get cranky and irritable when you're hungry, or when you eat junk you feel guilty and have negative thoughts about yourself? You're already down in the dumps, so don't exacerbate your bad mood through poor eating decisions. Though your world is turned upside down right now, when and what you eat is something you have direct control over.

This isn't a nutrition book, but I want to make a few comments about the food-mood connection and the fascinating relationship between your brain and gut. According to Dr. Vincent Pedre, author of *Happy Gut*, when we eat sugars, gluten, refined carbohydrates, and processed Frankenfoods, which are genetically modified foods, it negatively impacts the flora in our gut, which produce serotonin and dopamine—the neurotransmitters that make us feel happiness and pleasure. I was surprised to learn this, since I had assumed these neurotransmitters, which are also the same ones involved in the process of falling in love, were only produced in our brains. Certain fatty acids in the foods we eat and some gut hormones that can enter the brain impact our cognitive ability and can even affect learning, memory, and brain plasticity. What you're choosing to fuel your body with directly affects brain functioning and your mood.

The most devilish food is sugar because it feeds into the reward center of our brain and causes an emotional roller coaster. You've already hopped on this ride with the breakup, and eating high-sugar foods just increases your moodiness, irritability, and impatience, and is associated with depression and anxiety (as is gluten). Sugar also causes a biochemical inflammation that leaves your brain foggy and body achy. If you're thinking, "Screw the cupcakes, I'll just go for a cocktail," think again— alcohol metabolizes into sugar too. That's why you come back at night after drinking and raid your fridge for sweets—because your blood sugar has dipped and your body is craving more. So in addition to a hangover you're also feeling extra down and in a funk, since the sugar messed with the production of neurotransmitters.

If you're already feeling sad, demotivated, pessimistic, and lethargic from your breakup, I encourage you to be more thoughtful about what you put into your body. When making mindful food decisions, ask yourself where else you can find sweetness in your life that doesn't involve sugar. Loving and nurturing yourself in this difficult time can start with what you're putting into your body. If you're like me, a sugar addict, then you'll find the book *Body Love* by Kelly LeVeque extremely helpful in kicking your sugar crave-binge cycle so that you better balance blood sugar throughout the day and nourish your body with real foods. Of course, not everyone struggles with food choices, and the types and amounts of food will vary by your body type, your individual needs, and what feels right for you. The point is, be mindful of what you're putting into your body during this time of increased stress and make a conscious effort to make healthy choices that will leave you feeling good.

SLEEP: BEST BEDTIME TIPS WHEN YOU HAVE A BREAKUP ON YOUR MIND

So now that you know how important diet is, you're probably not surprised that there's a sleep-mood connection too. A lack of sleep can result in a mental state that resembles depression or anxiety, and people who are sleep deprived often report symptoms of irritability, hostility, low energy, and poor judgment. After a breakup, the stress and emotions can lead to short-term insomnia, with either difficulty falling asleep, frequent awakenings, or sleeping all day to avoid your new single life. Many times, racing thoughts about the breakup keep us up late at night. This impairment results in sleep deprivation and, often, disturbed daytime functioning, causing significant concern for those who are suffering. My friend, Dr. Clarisse Glen, board certified in sleep medicine, says, "On the bright side, these symptoms, however disturbing, are temporary and are expected to resolve once the 'stressor' resolves [in this case, the breakup] or the person adapts to the stressor. The best way to manage adjustment insomnia is to practice good sleep hygiene, relaxation techniques, and stimulus control. Medication is generally not recommended for treatment of adjustment insomnia, as the risk of adverse effects outweighs any potential benefit for a condition that is expected to be transient. Sleeping aids often cause residual daytime sedation, drowsiness, dizziness, cognitive impairment, and dependence."

You can combat sleep issues by creating a bedtime routine and setting a strict sleep schedule where you attempt to go to bed and wake up at the same time every day. Your bedtime routine should begin *before* you're actually ready to get into bed or fall asleep. This means taking a relaxing hot shower, picking out your outfit for the next day, putting on your PJs at a certain time, dimming the lights, listening to calming music, meditating, or reading a book. It does *not* mean falling asleep on the couch, stalking your ex on social media when you climb into bed, or wearing their old t-shirt as you cry yourself to sleep. You want your bed to be an ex-free, comfy, soothing space that helps you relax. One of the first things I did after my breakup—literally before I even moved out—was buy new bedding and throw pillows that I stashed in my trunk until I moved into my apartment. If it makes you feel better, buy a new mattress or bed. No need to hang onto things that remind you of your ex. This fresh start is all about you.

Best Bedtime Practices

✓ Avoid nightcaps—Although alcohol may help you zonk out, it negatively affects the restorative REM stage of sleep.

✓ Avoid caffeine—Don't drink anything caffeinated after 3:00 p.m., and be aware that caffeine can exacerbate anxiety.

✓ Avoid big meals before bed—If your stomach is growling, have a small, low-sugar snack.

✓ Avoid bright lights before bed and keep your bedroom as dark as possible—Turn off or dim overhead lights and use a low-wattage light an hour before bed.

✓ Keep the room cool with an open window, fan, or AC.

✓ Angle your clock away from the bed—Those glowing red numbers are only going to cause you anxiety when you count down the hours until you have to wake up.

✓ Keep your Bounce Back Journal next to your bed—Jot down any thoughts that are preventing you from falling asleep. Once you write them down, tell yourself that these are things to focus on tomorrow during your dwell spell (covered in chapter 6), but right now it's time for sleep.

✓ Try a deep breathing meditation using your breakup mantra (discussed in chapter 6), or listen to a soothing guided meditation.

✓ Don't hit snooze in the morning—You need to reset your circadian rhythm, so keep that schedule you set for yourself and get out of bed when your alarm goes off. A few days of waking at the same time can help reboot your body, and then if you're tired you'll have a better chance of falling asleep at a normal time the next night.

EXERCISE: SWEAT AWAY THE SADNESS

No more couch potato for you. If you didn't exercise before your breakup, you are now, and you can thank me later! Start small, then develop fitness goals to challenge yourself—you are going to feel amazing when you see progress, both physically and emotionally.

After my breakup I joined an MMA gym after stumbling upon a Groupon, and fell in love with a class that combines strength training, boxing, and kickboxing. I toned up, had increased energy and body confidence, and felt like I could kick ass, literally and figuratively, in my new life. The year following my breakup, I stayed committed to my workout and made a group of girlfriends who took the same classes as me. We started going out for sushi on Monday nights and gossiping about our love lives. It was exactly what I needed. If your social scene is directly tied to your ex, then meeting new friends through exercise will open up a whole new world of networking and social support.

Exercise Encouragement

✓ Buy fun workout clothes that make you feel good.

✓ Create an upbeat, empowering workout mix (none of the songs should remind you of your ex).

✓ Ask a friend to exercise with you, which also holds you accountable.

✓ Hire a personal trainer or join a fitness group that comes with an online support system (e.g., kaylaitsines.com, toneitup.com, crushfit.com, dailyburn.com, jillianmichaels.com).

✓ Before and after each workout, rate your mood 1–10 (10 = best), and keep an eye out for any patterns.

✓ Try new activities until you find something that feels more like play than a chore.

✓ Do a home workout on super busy days, even if it's just 15 minutes of plyometrics, abs, and push-ups.

✓ Keep in mind that you never feel guilty for exercising, you only feel bad when you don't.

I cannot stress enough the importance of healthy diet, sleep, and exercise routines to help regulate your mood when your reality has been shaken. There are so many resources available—books, websites, and apps that can educate, motivate, and hold you accountable. Consider hiring a specialist, such as a nutritionist or personal trainer, to give you personalized feedback and get you on the right track. On the flip side of things, it is possible to take your healthy habits to the extreme. Disordered behavior is more likely to begin during times of high stress and transitions. Be cautious about restricting food and overexercising, which can be a slippery slope. I promise you that the road to recovery starts with meeting your own needs—physical, emotional, spiritual, and environmental.

CREATING A NEW SENSE OF PURPOSE

Tied in with self-care is also the idea of creating a new sense of purpose. You're probably trying to figure out who you are after your breakup since it can be extremely jarring to split up and realize you lost yourself along the way. Your life is unbalanced right now, so the best way to get it back on track is to create a new sense of purpose. We do this by working toward new goals. Some of these may expand upon the skills you've been utilizing for self-care. Creating new goals will give you concrete direction in a time when you feel misplaced. Now is the ideal time to invest in your personal growth and development. Your relationship may have held you hostage in this regard, but now it's time to thrive! Grab your Bounce Back Journal and start brainstorming some projects, ambitions, and goals. The options are endless, you just need to get motivated and take the time to look into the possibilities. Aim for something challenging or slightly outside of your comfort zone for a boost in confidence and sense of accomplishment since your self-love tank may be running on empty these days. Your goals can be personal, fitness, or career oriented. What have you been dying to do? It could be working toward that big promotion or raise, going back to school or getting specialized training, signing up for an intramural sports team or race, a cooking or art class, learning a new language, creating a spiritual practice, or taking the trip to Thailand that you've always dreamed of. Solo, productive goals are great, but pursuing social activities that get you out of the house and mingling with other people are a good buffer to depression right now. Investing in these new goals and activities will help you put more energy and attention into other aspects of your life, creating the balance that you're lacking, and making the breakup feel less consuming. Your new purpose is part of a bigger self-love practice that you'll be doing while reading this book, and it'll bring you a sense of determination, self-reliance, and joy.

A SPECIAL NOTE ON FRIENDSHIPS

In my survey of people going through a breakup, I asked women to identify what they found most helpful in bouncing back from their heartbreak. The two most popular responses were quality time with friends and exercise. We covered the benefits of exercise, so now let's dive into the importance of friendship.

If all of your sense of self is still tied to your ex, then this is the crux of the pain. Your entire self-worth is wrapped up in the relationship from which you've just been rejected. Aloneness sparks our sense of fragility. In this vulnerable time, you may begin to believe that you really are worthless or unlovable. You might engage in the catastrophic thinking that you're doomed to be alone forever. This is when having a strong support network is essential because it's full of people who can show you that you still matter and that you still belong. Whether new or old friends, our breakup buds can reflect back to us a self who is worthy of love and acceptance, who is cared for and valued. When your self-esteem is at an all-time low, these are the people who can help empower you while you rebuild your self-worth.

Sometimes my clients tell me that they don't want to feel like a burden by asking for help. My response? Nonsense! True friends and loving family are people who genuinely care about you and who will be willing and honored to pick you up when you're down. If a friend were going through the same situation, wouldn't you be there for her? I realize not everyone has supportive parents or family members, so when I talk about a social network, choose the people who support you the most, who are on your team, who you can be vulnerable around, who you can laugh with, and who know the right things to say to boost your self-esteem.

Some breakup buds are good for lighthearted distraction, others for venting and serious emotional support. You'll want different types of encouragement at different times. Let your team know how they can best support you—do you want to laugh, do you want to complain, do you want words of wisdom, or just someone to sit on the phone and cry with you? Despite feeling alone, you don't have to go through this alone.

If your inner circle of soul sisters is low, it's time to reconnect. Maybe you alienated yourself from old friends when you were dating your ex. I think we are all guilty of drifting, especially when in a new relationship. But, it's always amazing how far a genuine "I'm sorry, I miss you and our friendship" can go. Many studies have also found that friendships increase our happiness. For instance, it's been found that the happiest people are the most social; if we surround ourselves with happy people, we're more likely to feel happy too; daily social support directly influences our feelings of optimism; and optimism has been shown to increase life satisfaction and lower our risk of depression.

MANAGING MUTUAL FRIENDS

Do you and your ex share a close circle of friends? You can't avoid everyone or throw them out in the trash with everything else that reminds you of your ex. It's unfair your heart is broken *and* you're the one now taking space from *your* friends, but you need distance so you won't be constantly reminded of your ex. No need to ditch all mutual friends, but it's important to acknowledge and discuss some breakup boundaries with them. People often forget while going through heartbreak that your friends and ex's pals you befriended were also invested in the success of the relationship (unless they hated your ex), rooted for the two of you to work out, and are experiencing their own mini loss. Though not as painful, there can still be a mourning period for *everyone* involved in this breakup.

How do you separate out this mess? If you brought your friend with you into the relationship, you get custody. If you befriended someone together during the the relationship, you get joint custody. If you have joint-custody friends, it's important to recognize the awkward position they're in. Address it with the following statement, "I know you're friends with both of us. I don't want you to feel like you have to choose between us. Can we set some ground rules so that it doesn't negatively impact our friendship?" See how your friend responds, then offer up suggestions on how they can best support you. You might ask your mutual friend not to mention your ex at all, or you may tell them you need to unfollow their account on Facebook because you don't want your newsfeed to be flooded with pictures of your friend and ex hanging out together. Remind your mutual friends they can still support you without ex-bashing. No need to call them names, or rant with you about how his new GF is fugly. They can check in about how you're feeling, rather than focusing on your ex's flaws. Your mutual friends might not want to be involved at all, so be respectful of these boundaries, and seek support from those who can provide it.

Creating a social network not associated with your ex gives you a sense of purpose and belonging during this chaotic time, when you're lost and struggling to figure out your new identity. A lot of people feel anxious forming new friendships, especially if they've had the same friendship circle for years, or don't know where to meet new people. If you're shopping for new breakup buds, break out of your daily routine and find new hobbies, activities, classes, or events with like-minded people. Search on meetup.com, eventbrite.com, or Facebook groups to find people with similar interests.

No surprise here that my favorite suggestion is to sign up for a fitness class. This is a bounce-back double whammy because exercise and quality time with friends are the two most helpful coping skills for getting over heartbreak. Try out a boutique gym, such as spinning, barre, or boxing, where you can go regularly and people start to recognize you. Say hello to the ladies sweating beside you, and take advantage of opportunities for conversation, such as asking someone how long they've been going to the gym, what other workouts they like, or where they got their cute workout pants. Take it outside of class by inviting folks for smoothies, or ask to go to a different class together. My own personal experience making postbreakup friends was that many women were hoping to create new connections but were too shy to "ask me out"—which is oddly similar to dating, probably because we all fear rejection. If working out isn't your thing, figure out what is—volunteering, book club, a wine-tasting series, flower-arranging class, acting at your local theater group, or playing in a new band. The secret is being assertive and putting in the effort to seek out new opportunities for connection.

HAVE AN ATTITUDE OF GRATITUDE

The last word or concept you're probably thinking about right now is gratitude. You're bitter, hurt, and wondering "why me?" But expressing gratitude is a secret weapon against misery. Gratitude involves being thankful, showing appreciation, and returning kindness. It's been shown through scientific research to increase happiness and optimism, decrease depression and anxiety, and even increase your quality and duration of sleep, as well as decrease the time it takes to fall asleep. With all of the benefits from fostering an attitude of gratitude, why not use it to get yourself out of a dark place?

In your Bounce Back Journal write down three genuine and specific things you're grateful for every day. Don't just write, "I'm grateful for my family." Instead, be more specific and write, "I'm grateful for the phone call with my mom this morning when she asked about how I'm doing." To reap the biggest benefit of your gratitude practice, focus on interpersonal interactions. This will help hold you accountable to reach out to your support network and decrease the social isolation that comes with depression. If you haven't had any recent personal interactions, practicing gratitude for other things is always better than not practicing at all, so take a moment to appreciate a beautiful sunset, a sparkly piece of jewelry, Amazon Prime, your pumpkin spiced latte, or the fact that you have legs and a beating heart. No matter your pain, being mindful and aware of even the smallest treasured moments can lift your spirits.

EXERCISE: WRITE A GRATITUDE LETTER

Write a gratitude letter to someone who helped you during this difficult time. I sent adorable friendship cards and handwritten letters to a few of my close friends who were really there for me. As you write your letter of authentic appreciation, imagine your friend's smiling face as they check their mailbox and open your card. Doesn't this give you the warm fuzzies, and something positive to think about? Tell your friend how much you appreciate her support and how she's impacted you.

CHAPTER 4

Tough Love for a Tough Breakup

You may not like what I'm about to share with you, but these tough love statements cut away the BS and tell it like it is. Fluff only has one place—well, two: on top of your ice cream sundae, or on a fluffernutter sandwich. There's no room for it in your breakup. So take your head out of the ice cream container, put your spoon down, and listen up!

This chapter is helpful when you've been triggered and have intense cravings for your ex. Many of these concepts are explored in depth throughout the book. Reread the chapter anytime you're lost in swirling, obsessive thoughts or relapsing into "I miss them" thinking. Let the quotes seep in, adopt some as affirmations, or save them on your phone for inspiration anytime, anywhere. Let's get started:

"Love is not a bargain."

You shouldn't have to convince someone to love you or be with you. Stop telling yourself if you did or said the right thing, your ex would choose you. Stop bargaining for scraps of someone. Stop settling for less than you deserve. Stop defining your sense of self by your breakup. Just because they rejected you, or the relationship did not turn out the way you planned, doesn't mean no one will ever love you. They're not the right partner for you if they can let you go. You may have spent more time in the relationship trying to please your ex, elicit praise, or keep them interested than being authentically you. Never bargain for love.

"You determine your own worth."

Your value doesn't stem from someone wanting to be with you. The breakup isn't about being prettier, smarter, or thinner. **You're enough.** If you don't love, value, or respect yourself, you won't find a partner who does, either. You attract someone who sees you in a similar light as you view yourself. You can sidestep old habits and create a new way of being and interacting—one full of self-love. It's time to reclaim your confidence, to tell yourself that you're enough in this moment, and to embrace who you are instead of trying to be someone else. Your value doesn't decrease based on your ex's inability to see your worth. Honor yourself, and the right person will recognize, support, and even enhance your qualities.

"By breaking up with you, your ex is choosing to live a life without you."

Ouch! I know that's like a dagger to the heart, but you need to hear it. If they can't appreciate you and think you're the best thing since self-serve frozen yogurt machines, then you're better off without them. Be with someone who can't imagine life without you. Your ex doesn't love you, or at least not in the way that you want/need to be loved. Having needs doesn't make you needy. You only feel needy when someone can't or refuses to meet your needs. Honor yourself and the way you want to be treated in life. Why would you want to be with someone who doesn't truly value you and recognize your worth? The only answer to that question is because you're not in love with yourself.

"The future you envisioned together is gone."

Poof! Just like that, the future you planned throughout the relationship is gone. Give yourself permission to mourn this loss—it's devastating and difficult to let go of the hope and excitement of a shared future. Sometimes the pain doesn't come from missing your ex, but rather the wound of being rejected, adjusting to change, and the fear of chasing your dreams on your own. After your mourning period, declare—or even celebrate (a happily-never-after party, anyone?)—a mental shift. Your thoughts control your reality, so your new mind-set should foster optimism for an unwritten future that can hold even greater love and happiness.

"Breaking up is part of dating."

The majority of your romantic relationships won't work out, that's part of dating. A relationship is still rewarding even if it comes to an end. Don't judge the health, happiness, and success of your relationship by the length of time it lasted, or allow it to be colored by what happened during the breakup. Get comfortable reflecting on the gray areas, without judging it as success or failure. Ideally, just one of your partners will remain in your life for the long run. Which means a fruitful dating life involves interacting with many partners and entering and exiting numerous relationships. Having this flexible mind-set allows you to adapt better, especially since over 40 percent of marriages end in divorce, and that's only those relationships that made it to the altar. Accept that breaking up is a natural part of dating.

"There are no failures in love."

You can view this relationship as a failure, or label it as an experience from which to learn and grow. Sometimes people serve us for a certain time or reason in our life, and just because the relationship ended doesn't mean it was a failure or a waste. It didn't turn out the way you hoped, but ask yourself: How was it successful? What was the value or silver lining you can apply to future love? Your only failure is not taking the time to learn from your love lessons. Collect as much dating data as possible after each date and relationship, which clarifies what makes an ideal match for you. Of course this also means examining how *you* could be a better partner too.

"If the effort isn't equal, it won't work"

One of you put in more effort to make the partnership work. Your relationship likely felt unbalanced. Were you a giver or a taker? A giver gives selflessly to make their partner happy, offering affection, acts of service, quality time, gifts, and praise in hopes of receiving reciprocal love. However, a taker focuses on meeting their own needs. Eventually the relationship ruptures. What needs

We have to stop asking
why this is happening to me,
and start asking
why it is happening for me.

AUGUST GOLD

weren't being met in your relationship? You shouldn't have to beg, nag, or demand a partner to put in more effort. In healthy relationships, you meet each other's emotional and physical needs through effective communication, compromise, and prioritizing each other's happiness.

"Actions speak louder than words."

The old adage is true. Your ex's actions were to break up with you, despite any confusing lines they might have fed you, such as "I'm not sure if I'm making a mistake," or "Maybe we can get back together down the road." They may still be texting you, or asking to hook up, but with no commitment. Unless they take significant action to rectify the situation, such as getting down on one knee, hiring your favorite singer to serenade you, or booking a couples therapy appointment, then don't cling to these words as glimmers of hope. Words are lazy, actions are meaningful. Exes have a magical ability to give you just enough to keep you holding on. Let go of these words because that's all they are!

"Sleeping together doesn't mean you're getting back together."

Using physical intimacy to get back into your ex's heart will likely only get you back in their pants. Though the breakup sex may be just as fiery as the argument that led to the split, sleeping together postbreakup, whether just one time or in a hanging-on hookup will not get you back to a happy, healthy place. Sex confuses things. We get lost in the love potion, a neurochemical response leading to a euphoric rush and clinginess when you separate. Women's sexual, emotional, and attachment needs are more closely related than they are for men, which means you're thinking sex can lead back to a relationship, while he's thinking this feels good in the moment. Using sex to manipulate your ex will likely backfire, leaving you feeling even worse. This is especially true if you used sex to gain intimacy instead of intimacy to gain sex throughout the relationship. Each time you're physical, it extends the breakup process and triggers more painful emotions, sustaining feelings of love that aren't reciprocated.

"You can't change your ex."

Sure, people can change. But unless you're a witch, magician, or voodoo practitioner, change has to come from within. No matter how much cheerleading or nagging you do, your ex has to want to change their behavior. My guess is that prior to the breakup you made your needs known. Though it may appear they weren't listening, they likely heard your requests and demands loud and clear. The frustrating part is that they'd rather break up than change for you. Save your breath and be with someone who wants to put in equal effort.

"You can't control other people."

Unfortunately you can't force your ex to say things or behave in certain ways. It's helpful to focus on what you can control, like your own behaviors, your reactions, and the ability to regulate your emotions. In terms of self-growth, you can work on increasing confidence, being a kinder person, making changes in your career, creating a more fulfilling life through hobbies and passions, living a healthier lifestyle through exercise and food choices, changing your personal style, and having a more positive attitude. Let go of what you can't control. Step into what you can control.

"Stop making excuses and set some breakup boundaries."

If your ex wants to talk to you or reconcile, they will. If they had the courage to end things with you, they can suck up their pride and beg for forgiveness. You don't need to get back your toothbrush. Stop hanging around their favorite bar hoping to bump into them. No more excuses, you must create space. Aim for *at least* a three-month no-contact rule. This is for your own sanity, and for your body to physiologically withdraw from love. It hurts immensely in the moment, but you'll heal more quickly as the weeks go by. The temptation to cyber-stalk them will nearly kill you, but I swear it gets easier. If you're hitting refresh every second on their status updates or looking for photo evidence of a new partner in their life, I might as well punch you in the gut, since you're clearly looking for pain. *Block, defriend, delete.* If you don't then all it takes is one glass of wine on a lonely Friday night and you're asking for regret! If you're really lacking control and willpower, there are apps you can download, such as SelfControl and Freedom, that allow you to block *yourself* from social media. Hide the sentimental photos and valuables away in your breakup box (discussed more fully in chapter 5) until you're emotionally detached.

"Having second thoughts doesn't mean
you should get back together."

Don't do anything rash. If you ended the relationship and are regretting it, take a deep breath and chill out. It's normal to miss someone who was a big part of your life, but you didn't make the choice to end the relationship lightly. There were legitimate reasons for the breakup. Don't put your ex on a pedestal, and don't be fooled by the pang of jealousy when they start dating again that you made a mistake. In your Bounce Back Journal, write down exactly why you ended it, and reread the list when you're having second thoughts to remember why you weren't satisfied. It's normal to feel annoyed and hurt that your ex's future partner will reap the benefits of all the hard work you put into "training" them on how to be a good partner. It would've been great if they got their act together while you were still dating or married, but this wishful thinking is toxic for your recovery. Instead of dwelling on why they changed for *her*, focus your energy inwards. What they do and who they date is no longer your concern. Investing in yourself and becoming the best version of you will help you reach the acceptance stage as you work through your grief. Once you realize and honor your worth, you won't care who they're dating because you'll be ready and open to attract a more ideal match.

"Even if you solve the breakup mystery,
the reality is that you're not together."

You can spend weeks or months of your life dwelling on what the hell happened. Some of the hardest breakups to comprehend were those without an articulated reason, or the explanation feels intangible—"I fell out of love." You can't vaporize your memories or compartmentalize such an enormous part of your life. Bottling everything up or engaging in negative coping skills such as self-medicating with drugs and alcohol or promiscuous behavior is harmful to your emotional and physical health. You may never get a straight answer from your ex, or the one you want to hear. Instead, create closure for yourself. This closure won't come from ruminating about their reasoning. Maybe you piece together it was due to conflicting desires for closeness and intimacy, misaligned core values, or love languages not being spoken. Take responsibility for your own actions, identify how these played into your false assumptions and internalized beliefs about love that stem from old emotional injuries (we'll explore this later), and commit to receiving love in a new way.

"You existed before your ex, and you will exist after them."

You're confused about your identity since you're not the person you were before the relationship, and you can't be the same person you were while in the relationship. Your self-concept has changed, and rather than fight change, give yourself permission to continue to evolve and grow. The relationship was a segment of your life, but it wasn't your whole world. Focus on creating new purpose, and treat this breakup as an opportunity to rediscover yourself—what *you* like, *your* preferences, and *your* opinions. Now is the time to develop your own life that's not in relation to a significant other.

"There's no crystal ball that tells you when you'll meet your ideal match."

The first person you date could be your lifelong partner, or the hundredth. We're all on our own unique journey. Stop comparing yourself to your friends, cousins, and everyone on Instagram. Let go of artificial timelines that cause overwhelming pressure. Take control of your love life by living authentically, getting clear on your core values, learning from your love lessons, showing up vulnerably on dates, analyzing your dating data to become a smarter dater, and not settling for less than you deserve. Anyone who tells you that you'll find love when you're not looking for it is wrong. It's a very intentional process. With every date and relationship experience, you should get closer to meeting your ideal match.

Are you able to see that this breakup is a blessing in disguise? If it's too early to find the silver lining, try a mental reframe by telling yourself that this experience is the greatest thing that ever happened to you. I know that may sound crazy right now, but viewing your breakup in this way opens the door for true transformation. Having faith in something means believing it's possible without having proof. If you believe there's a greater purpose in this experience, there will be. With some strength, hard work, and optimism, you will thrive. To continue employing the power of positive thinking, let's do a commitment exercise that can prevent emotional and behavioral backsliding.

EXERCISE: COMMITMENT CONTRACT

A contract can be a powerful motivator and carry a weight of importance. Create a self-contract, which is an agreement with yourself that will hold you accountable to your goals. Since life might feel overwhelming and unsteady right now, consider using a short-term contract that only lasts for a day or one week. That way you can change it as your goals shift, and you won't overcommit to an unrealistic goal and feel even worse if you break it.

In your Bounce Back Journal, write down some goals for how you want to treat yourself, or speak to yourself, boundaries you want to respect, or messages you want to keep at the forefront of your mind. Create a commitment contract with yourself around these ideas, taking into account your favorite excuses, negative self-talk, and behaviors that get in the way and prevent you from taking steps forward. It's best to focus on positive actions and outcomes. For instance, maybe you commit to certain acts of self-care, to prioritizing your emotional health, or to finding positive ways to comfort and support yourself in difficult moments. Use a format similar to the one below, or come up with your own:

I, _____ , hereby agree and commit to the following action(s) to improve my accountability to myself so that I can move on from my breakup, honor my worth, and take steps to create the love life that I desire and deserve:

1. _____

2. _____

3. _____

Sign: _____ Date: _____

For example, if you tend to verbally abuse yourself by calling yourself names, then you're going to commit to telling yourself how amazing you are, and reminding yourself that you're worthy and deserving of love. Or maybe it's your ex's birthday tomorrow, so you commit to ignoring them, instead coming up with a plan to pamper and distract yourself in healthy ways, such as by exercising, getting a massage, and having dinner with a friend. Try to be as specific and concise as possible, and make sure to sign and seal the deal. Respecting yourself enough to take this contract seriously is a great first step in rebuilding your confidence and valuing yourself.

CHAPTER 5

Cold Turkey Cutoff vs. Hanging-on Hookup

Based on my client work and survey of people going through a breakup, I found two distinct patterns of splitting up, which I have categorized into the *cold turkey cutoff* and the *hanging-on hookup*.

COLD TURKEY CUTOFF

As you've probably guessed, the cold turkey cutoff is when you have one or two breakup conversations and that's it—it's done! You might meet up once to exchange your belongings, but there is no ongoing flip-flopping about getting back together, or postbreakup sex. Even if the breakup conversation is a one-and-done, the pain can linger and keep you trapped from moving on unless you commit to working through it. People who experience a cold-turkey cutoff still go through the roller coaster of emotions and stages of grief. Like everyone else, they can be tempted to reach out to their ex in moments of weakness. So what's different about these people who don't get sucked into a hanging-on hookup situation? It can be a combination of things, including possessing personal qualities such as strong-mindedness; having positive beliefs about oneself, such as "I respect myself and won't continue to make myself vulnerable to someone who hurt me"; and being

43

savvy about self-care, especially turning to friends and family when in need of support and motivation, so that they don't cave and contact their ex.

Through my clinical work, I've found that people who cut things off cold turkey tend to make it through the healing process more quickly, especially if they had their questions answered in the final breakup conversation. This is in part because they are proficient at setting strong boundaries and are therefore not constantly triggered and relapsing back into contact with their ex. They also don't allow the breakup to define their sense of self, and have an easier time chalking up the relationship's end to the fact that it wasn't the right fit, versus the breakup being due to some inherent flaw.

That said, please note that there's a difference between taking your own personal time to thoughtfully process your breakup versus compartmentalizing the relationship and mentally vaporizing your ex, pretending they never existed to avoid processing any of your thoughts and feelings. If you're cutting-off cold turkey without doing the work, then all of the emotions and baggage may come back to haunt you later, such as by repeating negative patterns, picking the wrong partners, and self-sabotaging good relationships.

GHOSTING

Being ghosted is a type of cold turkey breakup, but it's one of the worst kinds because it happens without a word or explanation. If your ex ghosted, they literally went POOF and disappeared out of your life. You were totally blindsided, and this baffling breakup may have left you dying for an explanation. Are they really busy with work? Did they forget to tell me that they were going out of town to a land far, far away with no cell phone service? Did they get into an accident? Are they dead? Then the thought creeps in that he met someone else that he likes more. Your questioning quickly spirals and turns inwards. You're left to dwell and ruminate about what you did wrong, why you're not good enough, how you're flawed in some way, or why it was somehow your fault (all of which is not true!). Being left out of the blue is gut wrenching and traumatic. You obsess and overanalyze all of your interactions leading up to the disappearance. Not only do you waste your precious time thinking about the past, beating yourself up and feeling unworthy, but you waste your energy praying and hoping they will reach out in the future with a legitimate excuse so that you can discredit your theory that you're worthless and it's all your fault. Author Natalie Lue reminds us that "someone disappearing on you doesn't reflect your worth. It reflects their fear of being seen."

Research from the online dating site Plenty of Fish has found that of eight hundred millennial daters between the ages of eighteen and thirty-three, almost 80 percent of singles have been ghosted. This statistic is alarming. And what's even more concerning is that millennials who did choose to say something instead of ghost didn't handle it in a classy, face-to-face conversation either. In a 2014 study of 2,712 participants, 56 percent said that in the last year they had broken up with someone using digital media (texting, social media, and email), with texting as the most popular choice. Only 18 percent broke up in person, and just 15 percent picked up the phone to end the relationship. Interestingly, 73 percent of the survey respondents said they would be upset if someone broke up with them in the same manner. Sounds like people have forgotten the Golden Rule.

One of my clients, Hazel, came to me after a few years of unsuccessful dating. It turns out she had never gotten over her divorce and the fact that her husband ghosted her. Hazel was traveling for a teacher's conference when she came home to find her apartment empty and her husband nowhere to be found. For weeks she didn't hear from him, but knew he wasn't dead because his mother, who lived in a different country, reached out to let her know he was with her. He didn't return any of Hazel's calls and emails, and then two months later she was served with divorce papers. Turns out his family never accepted their marriage and had been begging him to leave her. Instead of communicating with his wife and working through these issues together, he took his family's side and completely abandoned her when she was out of town. What a devastating way to receive this news.

You may be tempted to reach out to find out what the heck happened and why your ex ended it in such a lame, cowardly way. In cases of ghosting or a short breakup text, your ex is likely immature and unable to identify, articulate, and communicate their feelings or reasoning. They may not be able to face breaking your heart, or are too self-absorbed to worry about your feelings and the impact ghosting can have. Though you may be tempted to text something like, "Hey asshole, ghosting isn't cool and you should have had the balls to end things to my face," it won't get you anywhere. Right now you're craving a sense of understanding, and want your confusion, anger, and sadness to be validated. Considering the way things ended, there's a high probability that they can't give this to you. You're probably not in a place where you can approach the conversation rationally and with the purpose of amends and forgiveness anyway, which you may be able to do in the future after completing this book. The urge to contact them will decrease, so in the meantime continue reading, complete the exercise in this chapter on creating closure, and focus on self-forgiveness. The reason *why* they ended it will become less important as you focus on the tools for healing yourself.

HANGING-ON HOOKUP

Where I see people get really stuck is in a hanging-on hookup scenario, in which it can take days, weeks, months, or in some cases years to really end things. This is a toxic and addicting cycle of communicating with your ex, where you struggle to cut the emotional cord. Whether it's texting, sleeping together, or a constant on and off again relationship status, it leaves you clinging to the hope that you can make it work. You waste a lot of time fantasizing that this time, it might be different; that it might work, only to feel disappointed and let down every time.

When you're in physical pain and bleeding, you take action to tend to the wound and heal it. You clean up the blood, put on a bandage, and are cautious about protecting yourself from reopening the injury and making it worse. Think of your breakup as an emotional wound. Every time you engage with your ex, it's like picking off the scab over and over again. Stop picking and allow the wound to heal. Time, space, and your self-care skills are a first-aid kit for your breakup.

Though there may have been a breakup conversation, or many, in your relationship, in a hanging-on hookup the reality is that you keep going back to each other for closeness, emotional support, physical affection, or sex. You continue to engage with your ex out of fear of truly letting go and living life without this person. You naively cling to the glimmer of hope that you'll sort through your problems and things will work out. I was a good example of a hanging-on hookup, where my ex and I lived together for three months after he decided that we weren't getting engaged, but still behaved as though we were a couple. If you're caught in this scenario, you may not be ready to walk away—you're likely stuck in the bargaining phase where you'll say or do anything to make it work. With this extended time together, it is likely an unhealthy roller-coaster ride. Oftentimes, postbreakup sex and temporary reconciliations just lead to the realization that it should have ended after that first breakup conversation. Don't beat yourself up if you've found yourself in a hanging-on hookup. It's an extremely emotionally taxing position to be in, and you probably handled it the best way you knew how at the time. But with the help of this book, you're going to start creating healthier boundaries and taking time and space to heal, during which you'll gain clarity about how you deserve to be treated.

Many people struggle to identify when to walk away, and how to call it quits. First, accept that just because a relationship *could* work, doesn't mean it *should* work. Stop trying to convince everyone else, and most importantly yourself, that your partnership was better than it actually was. You may be struggling with the idea of a fantasy relationship, one that's better in your head than in reality. Or the fear of failure, shame, and embarrassment keeps you clinging on for dear life, trying to prove it can work. Unfortunately, there is no one-size-fits-all advice for when to get out, unless there's physical and/or emotional abuse, in which case you should always get out as quickly as possible. Look out for someone whose anger is disproportionate to the issue that is frustrating them (explosive anger), and although not all substance users are abusive, it's a red flag to stick it out with someone who lacks control over substances and isn't taking steps to get help.

Both physical and emotional abuse can leave psychological scars. Physical abuse is more obvious, and occurs when your partner puts their hands on you (hitting, punching, pushing, kicking, pinching, slapping, etc.), causing harm and physical pain. It tends to happen during outbursts and in fits of uncontrollable anger. Typically in relationships with physical abuse there's also emotional abuse, but not always vice versa. Emotional abuse can creep up in a more insidious way. The victim doesn't always know it's happening because they minimize it, accept that it's just who their partner is, or start to believe they are flawed. *Gaslighting* is a type of emotional abuse in which you feel brainwashed and manipulated by your partner and start doubting yourself and losing sight of your identity. It occurs when you confront someone about their behaviors or the way you're feeling, and instead of acknowledging or validating your experiences, they somehow convince you that *you* are in the wrong, and *you* end up being the person to apologize. They flipped it on you, and you walk away upset and confused, or relieved to have ended the conflict.

My client Whitney was stuck in a hanging-on hookup for two years, and it took nearly two years of therapy for her to finally admit and accept that her ex was emotionally abusive. She rejected the label for so long because she couldn't stomach it. She didn't understand how a smart, confident, and strong woman like herself could be manipulated for so long. It didn't fit in with the life narrative she wanted, but she couldn't truly heal and move forward until she forgave herself for putting up with this behavior. Whitney recalled many small incidents, which in isolation didn't sound so awful, but when they were strung together she was able to see how he'd twist her words, discredit her reality, or not take responsibility for hurting her. One specific memory was when she snooped on his phone, looking for evidence, which she found, that he was secretly planning to see his ex-girlfriend behind her back. When Whitney confronted him about this news, citing a false source, he lied his way right out of it—even though she saw proof with her own eyes—and chose to believe him. These types of confrontations led to blow-out fights—the "shaking angry" kind—during which he'd call her psycho and crazy. Whitney said, "He denied me my right to my emotions."

Another powerful story of emotional abuse comes from my client Mary, who at the time of contributing this quote began exploring her divorce options.

Verbal abuse doesn't leave behind physical marks of pain, instead, it breaks your heart, bruises your ego, and shatters your self-worth. When my husband first started yelling at me, I thought it was an aggressive but relatively normal expression of frustration. People yell when they're mad, right? He'd tell me I was "crazy" with "psychopathic tendencies." Standing up for myself would only accelerate his anger until he would either blow up or storm out. He'd be extremely aggressive, or give me the silent treatment for days, always making amends on his timeline (usually with me apologizing for my behavior). Despite these gut-wrenching comments, he'd still say "I love you" and repeat it multiple times until I would hollowly say it back.

He also tried to cut me off from my support network so that I couldn't clarify if what I was experiencing was normal.

Only after much introspection did I realize that his attempts to degrade me were to cause pain and shatter my self-concept so that he could "win" and feel better about himself. The good news is that he shook my foundation, but never cracked it.

When he told me post partum that I didn't take care of my body, instead of crying in the corner I walked around the house naked eating ice cream because I am beautiful and free to make choices about my own body.

Emotional abuse is really about gaining control over you. It's a slow build of belittling and tearing you down, threatening you, diminishing your self-esteem, and eroding your self-worth over time. Below are some common signs of emotional abuse:

- ♥ Your partner controls who you spend your time with and manages how you spend your money.

- ♥ Your partner trivializes your accomplishments, puts down your goals, and calls you names.

- ♥ Your partner blames you for everything that goes wrong in your life together and rarely takes responsibility.

- ♥ Your partner constantly criticizes you, whether it's about how you act, dress, talk, or perform, and makes you feel like you're not good enough or flawed.

- ♥ Your partner manipulates you (sometimes by withdrawing affection or becoming emotionally distant) or forces you to do things you don't want to do.

- ♥ Your partner invalidates and refuses to recognize your emotional experiences.

- ♥ Your partner isolates you from friends and family.

*I will no longer
break my own heart—
to pacify the egos,
of others.*

TIFFANY AURORA

There's typically a cycle of abuse when the victim has had enough and decides or tries to leave, when the abuser suddenly becomes extremely sweet and apologetic, doting on their partner, and trying to make it up to them. This wooing behavior only lasts so long until trust is rebuilt, and then the abusive behavior begins again. If your partner tends to be controlling, manipulative (i.e., telling you they can't live without you or that you'll never find anyone else to love you), aggressive, or threatening, make a plan to leave. If you fear violence or retaliation, break up in a public place, have a trusted friend with you, or consider doing it via a letter or email once you've secretly removed your belongings from your home. Mentally rehearse what you're going to say so you can stay calm and it can just flow out of your mouth with no emotion (even if you're freaking out on the inside). Keep it short and firm, without room for negotiation or compromise, and focus on yourself rather than blaming or attacking your partner for their actions. For instance, "This isn't working for me. I can't continue to be in this relationship. It's over, I'm sorry." Buh-bye! If you're afraid to leave or need support around abuse, call the National Domestic Violence Hotline at (800) 799-SAFE (7233).

If you're stuck in a hanging-on hookup and need that extra push to end it forever, ask yourself if you like who you are in this relationship. If you don't like yourself or your behavior because you're feeling needy, crazy, jealous, insecure, anxious, or sad most of the time, it's a strong indicator that you need to walk away. Another is if you're constantly questioning whether this is the right relationship for you, or you're unsure if you can see a future together. If you've taken steps to clearly communicate and talk through your concerns with your partner without relief, clarity, or the necessary changes you need to see in order to stay together, then it's time to leave. For many people this breakup didn't happen out of the blue, and it's been a long time coming. You likely tried to work on the issues that were detrimental to the success of your relationship, so give yourself permission to close the door for good.

CLOSURE CONVERSATIONS

If the breakup took you by surprise and you weren't able to collect your thoughts or gain clarity, you may be craving a closure conversation. First, determine if you actually want closure, or if deep down you're hoping to rekindle or beg to get back together. A closure conversation isn't an excuse to convince your ex to give you another chance. The person who caused the pain can't be the one to support you right now. At best, they can acknowledge that they hurt you and apologize, but that's no guarantee. Again, I strongly recommend reading the rest of this book and waiting at least ninety days before considering whether or not you want to reach out. You'll gain ample understanding, insight, and knowledge along the way that will help you to create closure on your own. The risk of reaching out now is that your ex may ignore you and not respond, which can be even more hurtful. Plus, you might not like what they have to say, or in your mind their rationale still won't justify the breakup. To help you process this experience, let's do a two-part closure exercise.

EXERCISE: CLOSURE CONVERSATION

Take out your Bounce Back Journal and respond to the following questions:

- ♥ If I reached out to my ex, and they didn't respond to my attempts for a closure conversation, how would I feel? Would this put me in a better or worse place emotionally?

- ♥ What percent of me is secretly hoping my ex will want to get back together?

- ♥ What questions do I still have for my ex?

- ♥ Around what issues, topics, or conversations am I feeling the most confused?

- ♥ What specifically do I want closure around? (This could be your ex's reason for the split, past actions or hurts, or something they said during the breakup convo.)

- ♥ What could my ex say to bring me closure or greater understanding of the breakup?

- ♥ Why would these words bring me closure? How would they impact me, or be meaningful?

Next, I want you to try an exercise that may feel a bit silly or awkward, but instead of judging yourself just go with it. When you open yourself up to this exercise, you may be overwhelmed by just how powerful and emotional it can be.

Sit in a chair and place an empty chair in front of you. Imagine that your ex is sitting across from you and that this is your one opportunity to speak to them and ask the questions that have been burning in your mind. Picture what they look like, the expression on their face, what they're wearing, how they smell, and make eye contact with them. Really hold this image in your mind.

Ask your ex the questions for which you still need closure on that you identified above. Then, stand up and sit in the chair across from you, embodying your ex and responding to yourself as if you were them.

Because you've likely stewed over and hypothesized about your ex's responses to these questions before, rather than answering with what you *think* your ex would say, respond with what you *want* to hear that would bring you closure. Imagine how it feels for your ex to say these things, and the healing it brings you.

For example, during my heartbreak the most helpful thing I could imagine hearing was validation that our relationship was real and special to him even though it didn't work out, that I didn't do anything wrong, and despite moving on he'd never forget about me.

HOW TO GET FROM HANGING ON TO COLD TURKEY

The most important thing you can do to shift out of your hanging-on hookup dynamic is to cut off communication. I realize this is one of the most challenging aspects of a breakup. It feels like a gaping hole in your heart and your life. The person you used to snuggle to sleep, vent to about work, and text when you're bored is no longer your biggest support, confidant, and friend. I know one of the reasons you've stayed in contact is because of the hope of working it out, or fear of letting go, knowing each of you will move on with your lives, or that at least they will, and you'll be left behind. Believe me, I know how much it hurts to envision your ex with someone else, but you're also denying yourself happiness and new love by refusing to let go. By talking and texting and keeping each other as a constant in your lives, you're just delaying the inevitable and not allowing each other the space to heal. The hanging-on hookup is holding your heart hostage.

When my ex and I first broke up, my friend Jess kept telling me to stop communicating with him. I knew she was probably right, but I was afraid to stop because it meant that I really had to let go and focus on myself. Cutting cold turkey sounded so painful. I ignored her advice for a while, and would lie that I hadn't talked to him because I didn't want to disappoint her. But I was becoming acutely aware that I was stuck in the hanging-on hookup dynamic, taking one step forward and two steps back every time I heard from him. So, I reluctantly committed to no contact. I told him I was in too much pain, and I'd reach out in the future if and when I was ready to be friends, but in the meantime to please stop contacting me. It was like ripping off a Band-Aid, intense and agonizing in the beginning, but with time I stopped compulsively checking my phone, and day by day the no-contact rule became easier.

If you're stuck in a hanging-on hookup, believe in yourself that you have the strength to end it for good. You're no longer willing to settle for pieces of someone. Promise me that you'll stop engaging in any of the behaviors below:

BREAKUP DON'TS

- ♥ Beg/plead/bargain to get back together. You shouldn't have to convince someone to be with you or love you. The right person will not let you go.

- ♥ Drunk dial, text, or sext your ex. You'll regret it in the morning.

- ♥ Self-medicate with drugs/alcohol. The fleeting happiness and numbness might feel good in the moment, but trust me (as a clinician whose worked in the addictions field), you don't want to go down this path.

- ♥ Lure your ex back with sex. The physical intimacy won't mend your broken heart, and you're going to feel disappointed or guilty afterwards when you don't get what you really want.

- ♥ Rebound with every guy who shows you attention. Even if your ex didn't value you, you can still value yourself, and the beer goggles are seriously misleading you!

♥ Spend hours stalking your ex on social media. Compulsively watching their Snapchat and clicking on their Facebook page won't bring them back into your life, it triggers painful emotions, and you're just torturing yourself looking for traces of a new woman in their life.

♥ Hack into their email or voicemail. You'll feel worse and ultimately you want to be empowering yourself, not giving in to impulses.

♥ Show up at your ex's house unannounced. Hello stalker!

♥ Contact them in moments of weakness. That's what friends are for, so pick up the phone and call one of your breakup buds instead.

♥ Try to be best friends with them tomorrow. Lovers don't turn into platonic friends overnight, so let this idea go for now, and return to it when/if you're ready.

♥ Put your ex on a pedestal. In your mind, you may be highlighting all of their wonderful qualities, but there are likely many things that bugged you or you wish that you could change about them.

♥ Compare every new person you date to your ex. Unfortunately you can't take all of the things you loved about your ex and combine them with all of the things your ex was lacking to create a Frankenboyfriend. We'll visit this topic later on, but just know that when you open your mind to new people and experiences, you may surprise yourself with what you find.

The key to moving on is to minimize triggers in your environment and set healthy boundaries. To minimize triggers, set the following boundaries:

BREAKUP BOUNDARIES CHECKLIST

❑ If you're currently communicating, tell your ex that you need to stop, you're taking time and space to heal, and that you'll reach out when and if you're ready. Do not leave this up for debate, and do not feel the need to justify your actions or answer questions.

❑ Remove, unfriend, unfollow, or block your ex from all social media accounts, and no passive communication through "likes."

❑ Delete or hide virtual photo albums and pictures.

❑ Save your favorite images to a flash drive that you can put in your breakup box (described below) or give it to a trusted friend who will know the appropriate time to give it back.

❑ Delete your ex from speed-dial, remove their number from your phone (you can always keep it in your Bounce Back Journal), and block them when necessary.

❑ Donate, throw away, or put clothing, gifts, and other belongings that remind you of your ex in your breakup box (see Exercise: Create a Breakup Box on page 58). If these items are of value and you absolutely need to give them back, plan to drop them off when they're not home, or leave them outside your door where they can pick them up on their own schedule. If you must see them face to face, bring a friend with you so you don't get stuck engaging in yet another breakup conversation, bargaining to make it work, or having breakup sex.

❑ Stop going to cafés, bars, and restaurants where you think you might "accidentally" bump into them.

❑ Take space from mutual friends if needed.

❏ If their family reaches out, tell them you appreciate their support but you need to take some time and space to heal.

❏ Buy new bedding and change your pillowcase immediately so it no longer smells like them.

❏ Rearrange your furniture so it feels like a new space for this next chapter in your life, or rent a new apartment.

❏ If you share a child, it's best to create as amicable and respectful a breakup environment as possible. Consider consulting with a family therapist about best ways to coparent, and you may need to agree only to communicate about child-rearing issues at this time. There are a plethora of books on coparenting and how to minimize the damage of a separation on your child.

By recommending that you adhere to a no-contact rule and setting these firm breakup boundaries, I'm not saying you can never communicate with your ex again—just not right now, and not for *at least* ninety days. It's not realistic to be thinking about how to maintain a platonic, appropriate friendship right now. Even if you've reached the acceptance stage and have forgiven your ex, it doesn't mean you need to be friends. According to the 2016 *Singles in America* survey conducted by Match.com, only 42 percent of women would stay friends with an ex—the majority would not! You can always add this person back on social media or into your phone when and *if* you're ready to have a friendship down the road, but for now, no more excuses.

Of course there are some limitations to cutting your ex out of your life. If you have kids together, then of course you'll need to communicate to co-parent (never talk poorly about your ex to your child). In other situations you may work together, live in the same neighborhood, or belong to the same organizations and religious institutions, and it's not so easy or realistic to ignore then. You just need to be honest with yourself about why you're remaining in contact. Is it because you think you can convince them to be with you? Is it because you are afraid of being replaced or that they will forget about you? Are you still awaiting an apology for unfaithful or hurtful behavior? If you haven't already gotten the answers or outcome you've hoped for, then it's time to set your boundaries; otherwise you'll continue to feel dependent, needy, emotional, frustrated, and out of control.

EXERCISE: CREATE A BREAKUP BOX

Buy or repurpose a box where you can store keepsakes from your relationship. Toss in anything that reminds you of your ex that you're not ready to get rid of. Maybe it's a poem or sweet birthday card, an expensive piece of jewelry that you don't want to wear right now, or that flash drive of photos. Eventually you can house your Bounce Back Journal, and maybe this book too when you no longer need it. Keep it somewhere out of reach so that you put in effort to get it out. Tuck it deep underneath your bed, or buried in the back of your closet. Out of sight, out of mind.

Bonus points if you turn this into an extra-therapeutic exercise by converting an old shoebox into your breakup box. Flip through some magazines and cut out any words or images that represent your pain, your hurt, or the negative aspects of your relationship. Glue the images to the top and sides of the box. Psychologically, when you see the box you'll equate these negative feelings with your ex, and this can help prevent you from putting them on a pedestal or wanting to contact them. In fact, a study that recorded brain responses using an EEG found that thinking about your ex's negative features, though it temporarily may leave you feeling down, can blunt your feelings of love, so thinking these negative things may help you get over the breakup faster.

One day when it's less raw, you might want to fondly look back at the memories you shared with your ex, since after all, these experiences were part of your life. Or, maybe you're so blissfully happy in a new relationship or marriage that you never want to sneak a peek into that box, so you toss it out. The point is, I don't want you to be so impulsive that you destroy something you may want in the future. No matter what type of breakup you're going through—clean and immediate, or drawn out and messy—there will still be unresolved emotions and thoughts.

EXERCISE: UNSENT LETTER

WARNING: This can be a real tearjerker, but I promise it's cathartic and emotionally relieving. You are going to create an unsent letter to your ex. You have full creative rights here—it could be a traditional letter, beginning "Dear John" (or Dear Asshole), it could take the form of a poem, or if you're artistic you're welcome to let this take the form of a collage, painting, or drawing, which can utilize color and imagery to tap into emotion, or even write a song. Consider the following points to address:

- ❤ The anger, sadness, disappointment, or lingering emotions you have toward your ex
- ❤ The resentment or confusion for the way the relationship ended
- ❤ The loss of the future you didn't get to experience together
- ❤ The things you miss the most about them
- ❤ The things that drove you crazy about them
- ❤ The things you wish you had said to them
- ❤ The way you wish they had treated you

These are just some ideas to get your creative juices flowing. Put your pen to the paper and see what comes out. No need for perfection; let this be a judgment-free exercise where you can write anything without feeling ashamed, and no need to correct grammar and spelling. Once you're done, read the finished letter and allow whatever feelings to come up and flow through you, without the need to escape them.

The next step may sound dramatic, but you're going to destroy the letter. This can be something you do privately, or in the presence of someone else, such as your therapist or best friend. My personal favorite is to burn it—as you watch the flames engulf the paper, imagine the burden and weight of this breakup escape your mind and body. You are now free from this pain. If burning the letter is totally impractical, you can shred it into tiny pieces. As you drop each piece into the trash, imagine yourself letting go of a little bit of hurt, anger, and sadness. If you're not quite ready for destroy mode, you can keep the letter, and add to it and reread it as needed. Store it in your breakup box or leave it in your Bounce Back Journal. You may stumble upon it in a few months and be surprised by how far you've come.

CHAPTER 6

———————♥———————→

Get Out of My Head

After a big breakup you may constantly feel on the verge of freaking out, like you could lose it at any second. Your ex is running a marathon in your mind. You can't get them or the breakup out of your head and it's driving you cray cray. Have no fear, this is actually normal. I repeat, *normal*! You are human, and as a human, it's natural for your mind to race and thoughts to come in and out. Ruminating and obsessing is a way we deal with big changes. This breakup just rocked your whole universe—of course you're going to dwell on it.

Women tend to ruminate and obsess, while men are more likely to distract and avoid. This may help explain why two days later he's at the bar with his friends acting like nothing happened, and you're at home bawling your eyes out. You'll cycle between being able to distract yourself, and feeling overwhelmed and flooded by emotion. To better understand the breakup process and what's happening, let's look at the brain and the neuroscience behind why heartbreak is so freakin' hard to overcome. What you learn will hopefully put your mood swings into perspective and allow you to be more compassionate with yourself.

YOUR BRAIN ON A BREAKUP

I want to help explain to you *why* it's been so challenging to let go and move forward. The answer has to do less with your ex being your perfect match and more to do with neuroscience! Before you tune out because I just said the word *neuroscience*, stick with me here because this insight can change the way you conceptualize your entire breakup pain.

A breakup impacts us on a neuropsychological level, similar to drug withdrawal. But, to understand your brain on a breakup, you first have to understand how *love* works. Dr. Helen Fisher, Chief Scientific Advisor at Match.com, found through functional magnetic resonance imaging (fMRI) that participants who reported themselves as being deeply in love had the same brain region light up that is linked with addictions to substances such as nicotine and cocaine. The dopamine released in this reward center is very pleasurable. In her book *Anatomy of Love*, Dr. Fisher explains that, "men and women who are intensely and happily in love are addicted to their partner." She describes that romantic love isn't just a feeling, it's a drive, a motivation to get a preferred mating partner. She states, "Romantic love is like thirst, and our lover is water, we are driven to them." Basically, love is a positive addiction, but we withdraw from love similarly to how we withdraw from other addictions—painfully.

When first falling in love, we experience both physical and emotional responses, such as sweaty palms, flushed cheeks, racing heart, passion, anxiety and preoccupation with our new partner caused by an increase in the stress hormone cortisol, which lowers levels of serotonin, which is responsible for those obsessive, infatuated thoughts. That's why in the beginning of your relationship your new partner is constantly on your mind. You might catch yourself smiling and daydreaming about them, or a friend might tell you that you're glowing. Other chemicals involved in romantic love are vasopressin and oxytocin, responsible for feelings of attachment. There's the saying "love is blind" because some of the neural responses during new love actually shut down our ability to make judgments and critical assessments about others. That's why when we fall in love in that early honeymoon phase we miss a lot of red flags, and we think our partner is perfect!

Dr. Fisher's groundbreaking research about how our brain processes rejection helps explain the obsessive behaviors and depression that we experience in heartbreak. If you look at love through an addiction framework, when you split up and cut off communication and physical touch, your brain goes through withdrawal—similar to withdrawing from drugs. Your brain says, "Where'd my lover go? I *need* them to feel good." Your body and brain have grown accustomed to getting their daily "hit" of love, romance, and affection, and now it's gone. The pleasure center of your brain is no longer producing a rush of dopamine that gives you that excited, lovin' feeling, and the oxytocin released from their warm touch is no longer soothing you. There's a real physiological response to this change in your life. You're now left craving your ex, wanting to get your next fix.

Common withdrawal symptoms in both love and drug addiction include difficulty sleeping, crying, anxiety, changes in appetite and eating behaviors, and depression. You can be triggered by people, places, and things, such as mutual friends, songs, recipes, and smells. These cause intrusive thinking, missing them intensely, and acting impulsively, such as by showing up at their apartment unannounced or compulsively texting ten times in a row despite no response. When I used to see the same type of truck my ex drove out on the road, I'd think it was a sign that we were supposed to be together and then I'd miss him like crazy. What impulsive things have you been tempted to do, or even done, in the despair of these withdrawals?

In her study "Reward, Addiction, and Emotion Regulation Systems Associated With Rejection in Love," Dr. Fisher and her colleagues took brain scans of ten women and five men who had recently been rejected by a partner and reported they were still intensely in love and spent the majority of their time thinking about their ex. When asked to look at a photo of their rejecter, the participants reported feeling love, despair, both good and bad memories, and wondering why this happened. The results showed brain activation in several regions of the reward system, including areas associated with romantic love (the ventral tegmental area), attachment (the ventral pallidum), and anxiety, physical pain, and the distress associated with physical pain (the insular cortex and the anterior cingulate), as well as areas associated with cravings, addiction, and assessing gains and losses (the nucleus accumbens and orbitofrontal/ prefrontal cortex). It's fascinating, but intuitive, that breakups tap into the part of the brain that processes the distress associated with pain—hello zombie mode! No wonder why I felt extremely exhausted and as though I'd been punched in the gut during those first few days of my big breakup. When these brain regions are activated, your body thinks something bad just happened to it, and this can lead to the release of stress hormones.

There's even something called "broken heart syndrome" (officially called takotsubo cardiomyopathy), which is when the heart is weakened under intense emotional stress, and in rare cases has even led to death. In other words, both the psychological and physiological distress you're under during a breakup is very real.

Coinciding with the five stages of breakup grief that I discussed in chapter 2, in *Anatomy of Love* Dr. Fisher identifies the following breakup phases based on what happens in our brains:

- ♥ **Protest Phase** (similar to the bargaining stage): You work obsessively to regain your ex's affection. As despair sets in, you give up hope and slip into depression.

- ♥ **Frustration-Attraction Phase** (similar to the denial stage): Your passion intensifies when your needs aren't met and you face barriers to your romantic feelings. When the reward of being with your lover is delayed, the brain's dopamine system still continues to be activated, which sustains your feelings of intense romantic love, even though you're no longer with your partner.

- ♥ **Frustration-Aggression Phase** (similar to the anger stage): You feel anger and hostility in response to being abandoned. The rage system is connected to centers in the prefrontal cortex that anticipate rewards. When you realize that you're not getting the reward (being with your ex), these brain regions stimulate the amygdala and trigger rage, which also stresses the heart, raises blood pressure, and suppresses the immune system.

- ♥ **Resignation/Despair Phase** (similar to depression stage): You give up pursuing your ex and experience a decrease in energy, pervasive sadness, hopelessness, and depression (a more intense version of Fisher's protest phase). As you accept that the reward will never come (you're not getting back together with your ex), dopamine-producing cells decrease their activity, resulting in lethargy and despondency. Long-term stress suppresses the activity of dopamine and norepinephrine, resulting in depression instead.

These stages help to explain why you can't seem to let go, and all you can do is think about your ex. Your brain is driving you to sustain feelings, even though intellectually you know that the relationship is over. I hope that reading and understanding how your brain functions during a breakup provides validation for your distress, and puts your intense feelings into perspective. Don't misattribute this pain to the conclusion that your ex must have been The One. This will only lead to mistakenly placing even more meaning and importance on your ex and the relationship. Rather, I challenge you to more realistically reframe your current pain as a *physiological response to withdrawing from love*. When you think of your pain in this way, it gives your ex less power over you. Yes, you were in love with a specific person, but your body is wired for connection, and this is the general response it goes through when the love is taken away. Less emphasis here on your ex, and more about what's happening in your body.

BREAKING THE ADDICTION

Now that you know love is an addiction, and the withdrawal symptoms you're experiencing are neuropsychologically justified, you can understand why setting firm breakup boundaries and minimizing the triggers in your environment are essential to your recovery. Finding your ex's sweatshirt at the back of your closet or seeing them pop up in a mutual friend's Snapchat can send you spiraling into a relapse resulting in reaching out to them. When they don't respond, you may feel upset for still caring, or obsess over why they haven't gotten back to you, which feels awful, like a breakup "hangover." Lacking control during this highly vulnerable time is when you're likely to reengage in hanging-on hookup behavior—bargaining, begging, or banging your way back together, only to be disappointed and go through the grief process all over again. You're likely in the frustration-attraction phase, where your cravings and passion are intensified because you've had a little bit of contact with your ex. Whether it was sleeping together or just meeting for coffee, your brain is continuing to sustain those unrequited feelings of love. Take the steps to help your brain chemistry chill out by taking space to emotionally and physiologically move through the breakup phases. The cold turkey cutoff approach gives your body time to heal on its own. Eventually your love will burn itself out.

FIND MINDFUL MENTAL RELIEF

You're now committed to no contact and cutting off communication, but the ruminating and dwelling has nearly taken over your life. How can you find relief? It's all about being mindful. You've probably heard the buzzword "mindfulness" a lot lately, but unless you practice it, you might not even know what it means. You don't need to be a monk or hippie to practice it, and you don't need to wear yoga pants or contort your body into weird poses to have mindful moments. Mindfulness is a heightened state of awareness where you're solely focused and grounded in the present moment. It's about gently acknowledging your automatic thoughts as they come in and distract you, letting them go and returning to your conscious awareness. It's powerful to realize you actually have control over your thoughts, and that you can choose whether or not you want to engage in them.

In regard to your breakup, the first step of mindfulness is being aware when you're thinking about your ex or ruminating about how you'll never get over them. We have automatic thoughts all of the time that race through our minds, but we aren't always tuned into them. It's the moment you step away from those thoughts, realizing that you just spent ten minutes stewing that is the pivotal moment in which you have a choice to continue to waste your time on thoughts that keep you down, or redirect your consciousness.

If you're new to mindfulness, it's easier to start by noticing your downtrodden mood or behaviors first and working backwards. For instance, you might catch yourself typing your ex's name into the Instagram search bar, but how did you get there? You're then able to trace this behavior back to the fact that you were thinking about that time you went to Costa Rica with them and how you can't believe you'll never be on a vacation together again. Ideally, with a mindfulness practice, you won't even get to the point of looking them up on IG because you'll already be aware of those initial thoughts and change the course of your actions. Choosing whether or not to engage in a thought is the glorious thing about being present and mindful, redirecting your thoughts to only those that serve you!

Honor the space
between no longer
and not yet.

NANCY LEVIN

Visualization can also be a helpful tool. When you become conscious of your thoughts, allow your negative obsessions to drift away, like a cloud passing in the sky. Your ex is a big dark cloud, looming overhead, blocking your sunshine. Let that cloud pass, so that the strong rays of sunshine can warm your body with positivity. You can also imagine yourself holding a balloon, which represents your thought. Let go of the balloon, watching your thought drift off into the sky. Or imagine yourself as a passenger in a car. The scenery outside of the window represents the thoughts and memories of your ex. You can focus on one item, or allow it all to pass by in a blur, detaching from the distracting thoughts. I liked to pretend I had on boxing gloves and imagined myself punching away each negative thought, with the face of my ex on it. You can even make a sound effect—hiya!

MEDITATE YOUR WAY TO PEACE OF MIND

Meditating is about being in the present moment, clearing your mind from racing thoughts when they swoop in and distract you, and tuning into your physical body and breath. It's about stringing together these mindful moments and noticing when your consciousness has shifted elsewhere. Being distracted by a thought is not failure; it's part of the process. When this happens, practice one of the visualization techniques I just described. You'll become a mental ninja—thoughts won't be able to sneak up unannounced and hurt you.

Meditation is effective in managing and easing stress and anxiety. It's a lifesaver when you're in the early stages of the breakup process, when it's so painful you feel like you are living minute to minute and can't let your obsessive thoughts go. Though you may tend to reject feelings or try to run from them, allow yourself to really feel and sit with mixed, difficult emotions in a safe space, which will attune your mind and body in an accepting and compassionate way. Similar to how labeling your emotions can help decrease their power and intensity, meditating by asking yourself what you're feeling and then recognizing and welcoming the variety of emotions flooding through you can be cathartic as well.

To reap the benefits of meditation, you must practice it regularly, making it part of your daily routine. Start small with just two to five minutes per day, then increase the amount of time as you improve, perhaps to twenty minutes per day. Two minutes is always better than no minutes! Your goal should be no thoughts about your ex for just the time you're meditating. Expecting them to completely disappear from your thoughts is unrealistic, but having them out of mind for even a few minutes can be a much-needed mental vacation. Notice that by simply closing your eyes and taking a deep breath you can escape from external stimuli and feel a sense of calm rush over you.

Begin using this new coping skill right now by downloading a user-friendly app such as Calm, Headspace, 10% Happier, or Buddhify. Deep breathing, guided visualizations, and progressive muscle relaxation are good places to start in Google search. Pick one that works for you.

EXERCISE: CREATE YOUR OWN BREAKUP MANTRA

A mantra can be any sacred word that is used as an object of concentration and embodies some aspect of spiritual power or sense of peace. Similarly, an affirmation is a positive, true statement that you can make about yourself. Meditating with a mantra balances your central nervous and endocrine systems, and can create a deep sense of relaxation. I want you to choose a personalized breakup mantra or affirmation, used to soothe and regulate your emotions and empower you. Here are some suggestions, or come up with your own:

- ♥ Strength
- ♥ Resiliency
- ♥ Acceptance
- ♥ Forgiveness
- ♥ Kindness and compassion
- ♥ Healing and growth
- ♥ Embrace change
- ♥ Choose happiness
- ♥ Bounce back
- ♥ Give and receive
- ♥ Unlimited potential

- ♥ Replace anger with love
- ♥ My pain is wisdom gained
- ♥ I love myself
- ♥ I deserve love
- ♥ I am enough
- ♥ I am worthy
- ♥ I am lovable
- ♥ I am at peace
- ♥ I am a catch
- ♥ I am loving and loved by many
- ♥ I set the standard for how others treat me
- ♥ She needed a hero, so that's what she became

Pick whatever you connect with and doesn't make you feel too cheesy! To be honest, I used to hate affirmations because I didn't *believe* them. I was operating from a place of doubt and limiting beliefs. But after reading, learning, and doing more research about them, I realized they're basically a cognitive therapy tool, with a little extra feel-good *umph*. Affirmations bridge the gap between therapy and spirituality. If you believe the message you're putting out into the universe, or at least desperately want to believe it, then this faith will help change the course of your reality. That's because your thoughts impact your mood, which impacts your behavior and actions, which change your reality. Allow yourself to really feel the affirmation in your body; it should fill you with a sense of excitement, hope, and optimism. Write down your mantra or affirmation in your Bounce Back Journal, on a Post-It stuck to your bedroom mirror, or on a bookmark for this book. You want to constantly be reminded of this positive thought, and it should become a ritual in your day. You can say your mantra out loud as part of your mindfulness or meditation practice, in the mornings when you first wake up, while you're washing off your makeup and looking in the mirror, or when you climb into bed at night.

EXERCISE: DEEP-BREATHING WITH MANTRA

Let's combine your breakup mantra with a deep breathing meditation. First, read through the exercise so that you understand what to do, then put down the book and practice it before heading to the next chapter.

1. Make sure you're sitting in a comfortable, upright position, relaxing into the chair or bed that supports you so that you can release any unnecessary body tension. Close your eyes gently.

2. Take in a few deep, restorative breaths at your own pace.

3. Tune into your body, and ask yourself what you are feeling. Distance yourself from your automatic desire to intellectualize or think, and simply listen to what your body is saying. Take a few moments to tune in.

   It's easier to first figure out where your emotions are hanging out. Some people experience emotions in their chest. What emotions may you be holding there that are making it difficult to breathe? Others clench their fists, holding onto tense or angry feelings. Some feel stress and heaviness in their shoulders, as if they're being weighed down. You may feel like something is dancing around in your stomach, which is a common location for nerves and anxiety. These are only suggested feelings and locations; there's no right or wrong sensation or emotion. What is your body telling you?

   Once you've located where your feelings are living inside of you, attune to what each unique one is saying. As you identify and label each emotion, think or speak out loud the following statement: "I will honor my feeling of _____." Tenderly welcome each emotion without judgment.

4. Once you've labeled and honored each emotion, you'll begin mindfully breathing. Breathe in a 1:2 ratio, breathing in through your nose for four seconds, hold for a brief pause, and then exhale with a whooshing sound for eight seconds.

5. At the end of your exhale, speak your breakup mantra out loud in a confident voice.

   Breathe in for 4 . . . out for 8 . . . say your mantra.
   As you're breathing in, focus on feeling the air move from your nose, down through your throat and chest, filling your belly, even moving down through your toes.

6. Imagine the air is full of healing power. You're inhaling peace, strength, and positivity and you're breathing out tension, negativity, and pain. With each deep restorative breath, your heart heals a little bit, and you let some of the anger and sadness go, or whatever emotions you no longer wish to hold onto. Imagine your body feeling lighter with every breath, and the weight of the breakup decreasing with every exhale.

7. Continue breathing in for four seconds and out for eight for a total of ten more grounding and restorative breaths. Remember to repeat your mantra or affirmation at the end of every breath.

   Breathe in for 4 . . . out for 8 . . . mantra x 10

8. Before opening your eyes, realize that you have the ability to soothe and comfort yourself. That there's a stable part of you that can step back from the pain, and tend lovingly to the parts of you that are writhing in agony. With compassion, you can nurture the hurt parts and feel competent that you're attending to your own needs.

Use this meditation and mantra any time you notice those obsessive thoughts swirling around in your mind, or the storm of emotions becoming too great. Visualize letting go of your distracting thoughts and tune into your physical body for a few stress-free moments of peace. Live fully in the present moment. Just breathe. Ahh, doesn't that feel better?

The next exercise will get your creative juices flowing! Taking meditation one step further, you're going to write and record your very own personalized meditation that you can listen to whenever you need it. This exercise shouldn't be rushed, so make sure to carve out time when you can brainstorm, and tap into your creativity.

EXERCISE: WRITE AND RECORD YOUR OWN MEDITATION

Before writing your meditation, here are some questions to consider:

- ♥ What do you hope to accomplish by listening to your meditation?
- ♥ Do you want to relax?
- ♥ Do you want to stop thinking about your ex?
- ♥ Do you want to feel empowered?
- ♥ Do you want to tune into your emotions?
- ♥ Do you want to recognize what you need in this moment?
- ♥ Do you want to ditch your negative thinking?

Take out your Bounce Back Journal and write whatever supportive, soothing, encouraging statements come to mind. Perhaps it's a list of your favorite affirmations, a pep talk about all of your own wonderful qualities, some lines you love from your favorite motivational and inspirational speaker, or how you're taking control of your life.

This is *your* meditation, so it's totally up to you what to include. Once you've written it, I want you to record yourself reading it (most iPhones and Androids come with a voice recording app installed), so that you can listen to it whenever and wherever you are. Think about how powerful it is to hear your *own* voice guiding you through difficult moments, cultivating self-worth and strength during this difficult time.

USE A DWELL SPELL

Another mindfulness coping skill to control your racing thoughts is creating a dwell spell—a limited and structured time during which you have permission to let your mind go crazy. You have control over how long or short it will be. At the beginning, all-consuming stage of your breakup, you may need a significantly longer dwell spell. Try two hours per day and see how that feels. You can break down the two hours into half-hours or fifteen-minute sessions spread throughout the day if your mind is really racing. The rest of your day, however, is devoted to being in the present moment and creating the life you want to live. Over time, give yourself shorter and shorter time frames in which to ruminate. Don't be afraid to challenge yourself.

Set strict boundaries by setting a phone alarm that will alert you to the beginning and end of the dwell spell. For example, from 6:00 p.m. to 8:00 p.m. you have permission to ruminate and obsess about why it ended, or wherever your mind takes you, but when the clock strikes eight, pack those distressed thoughts away until your next worry period. It's helpful to identify an activity you're going to do at the end of your dwell spell so that you have a plan for a smooth transition—cooking dinner, calling a friend, or turning on a favorite show that will distract you.

In your Bounce Back Journal, add a dwell spell section where you can jot down what thoughts or emotions bubble up throughout the day. Now that you're practicing mindfulness and meditation, you'll be more aware of your intrusive thinking. Once these thoughts are on paper, you can freely move on with your day knowing that you can revisit and fully explore these thoughts and feelings later on within your limited dwell spell. You might be surprised to find that these notes feel like old news just a few hours later. The key is to be strict with yourself about only dwelling during the allotted time. Keep in mind the wise words from Eleanor Roosevelt: "With the new day comes new strength and new thoughts."

CHAPTER 7

Understanding Your Breakup

In the haze of your breakup, the biggest question burning in your mind is probably "Why?" Why did this happen to me? Why didn't the relationship work out? Why are they leaving me? Why didn't we try harder? Why did they fall out of love? Why were they unfaithful? Why did we want different things? Why won't they change? Why did I mess this up? Why did I push them away? Why do I always screw everything up?

You question who's at fault and what you could have done differently. You're grasping for some explanation or reasoning. If it was a totally one-sided decision, the lack of control and unjustness of the situation is turning over and over in your mind. It's annoying, yet normal, to replay every conversation, every date, every moment—scouring through past texts and e-mails. You're looking for breakup evidence—something black and white that went wrong. You want to put your finger on the turning point, or identify what couldn't be fixed.

The most frustrating part of the breakup is the constant questioning, and ruminating over what happened. You cling to the words your ex said in their breakup speech (or lack thereof), looking for clues. Though there are many different reasons for a breakup, research found that being rejected for someone else hurts most because of the sense of exclusion and decreased belonging. In breakups without reasons, like ghosting, researchers found that your default is to assume you're being left for someone else. If your ex insists there's no one else in the picture, then this lack of a clear-cut reason keeps you obsessing. You could spend the rest of your life searching for the breakup evidence. You may never find it. Reasons help us rationalize and intellectualize the pain we're experiencing. But here's a caution: demanding reasons or repeatedly rehashing the same points over and over again is where you'll waste the most time in getting through your breakup. Don't get stuck here! You could spend years guessing your ex's emotional experiences and choices, but girl, you have better things to do. Plus, whatever the reason for the breakup, your ex ultimately does not want to be with you, otherwise you'd be in a relationship. They're choosing to live life without you by their side, and as painful as this is, it should serve as a wake-up call that you deserve someone who cannot bear to live without you.

My goal is to help you gain insight and identify foundational problems that were lurking beneath the surface of the relationship that perhaps you didn't realize you had, or that you intuitively felt but couldn't articulate. These are usually the mysterious underlying reasons for the "It's not you, it's me," or the "I fell out of love" breakups. As we explore these reasons, don't hesitate to put your own behavior under a microscope in the service of learning your love lessons. Below are some reasons that may explain why your ex wasn't your perfect match.

GENERAL REASONS FOR A BREAKUP OR UNDERLYING RELATIONSHIP DISSATISFACTION

- ♥ Differing needs for intimacy and conflicting attachment styles
- ♥ Love languages not being spoken/received
- ♥ Differing core values
- ♥ Incompatible personalities
- ♥ Issues around conflict resolution and communication
- ♥ Inability to receive your partner's affection due to past emotional injuries and destructive, deep-seated internalized beliefs about yourself and love

If you're in the dark about the breakup, your ex probably:

- ♥ Can't identify their feelings or communicate clearly

- ♥ Made a statement such as, "It's just a feeling, I might be making a mistake"

- ♥ Avoids confrontation, doesn't answer follow-up questions, ignores you, or becomes defensive when you ask for an explanation

- ♥ Refuses to take responsibility for their role in the breakup

- ♥ Feels sorry for themself, saying, "You deserve better, I'm holding you back"

- ♥ Shuts down and withdraws emotionally—the more you push, the more you are ignored

- ♥ Gets angry, aggressive, and argumentative, with yelling, name calling, or blaming you for all of the relationship problems

Taking all of this into account, you may not be as much in the dark as you previously thought. Often, your partner either directly told you how they felt, or they gave you hints that something was wrong or changing.

EXERCISE: UNCOVERING BREAKUP EVIDENCE

Looking back at your relationship, answer the following questions in your Bounce Back Journal:

- ♥ Over the course of your relationship, what major problems or concerns did you talk about and effectively work through together?

- ♥ What issues existed in your relationship that were never resolved?

- ♥ What warning signs did you ignore in the relationship?

♥ What would you rate your overall relationship satisfaction from 1 to 10 (10 = most satisfied)? What number do you think your ex would rate it? Did this number shift significantly from the beginning to the end of your relationship? What about day to day?

♥ Did your ex address any problems or concerns in the weeks or months leading up to the breakup?

♥ Did you act or behave differently leading up to the breakup? Did you notice any changes in their behavior?

♥ For which problems, dissatisfactions, or conflicts can you take responsibility? How did your behavior contribute to the breakup?

TAKING A RELATIONSHIP INVENTORY

Once a relationship ends, you may not get any further explanation, and obsessing over their thoughts and motivations won't help you move forward. Self-reflection is key to take back control. This is not about blaming yourself, but rather about learning from your experiences and finding room for improvement. You can't control how your ex behaved or their decisions, but you do have control over using this experience as an opportunity for growth. This isn't about accusing yourself, but rather about finding ways to improve the next time around (because none of us are perfect!).

Leading up to the breakup, you may not have liked what your ex had to say, so you blew it off and didn't take their requests or demands seriously. Maybe you refused to change. When you objectively look at your behavior, you may be able to identify your role in the outcome of the relationship. Maybe you were the one to resist commitment, to cheat, to struggle with addiction (to love, drugs, or alcohol), to have unrealistic expectations or be too demanding, to criticize, yell, belittle, and break your partner down. It's important to turn inwards, acknowledge, and claim responsibility for your mistakes. We all make them.

My client Sarina was able to take a relationship inventory, acknowledge her wrongdoings, and create closure for herself. After three years of marriage, her husband, Jerry, asked for a divorce after discovering that she was having

Sometimes it takes a
heartbreak to shake us
awake and help us see
we are worth so much more
than we're settling for.

MANDY HALE

an emotional affair. Sarina said it was easier for her to receive sympathy from her family and friends than deal with the shame and guilt that she bottled up around her own actions. In exploring her marriage, Sarina identified a multi-year decline in attention and effort by *both* partners. However, at the time of her affair she felt justified in her actions because she put the full blame on Jerry, feeling bitter and hurt that he let them grow apart. In our work, Sarina realized that instead of turning to him any day over that last year to express her concerns or address how she was feeling, she invested her time and energy outside of their relationship. Whether or not there was infidelity in your relationship, the purpose of this example is to highlight that there are likely things that you can take responsibility for in regard to the downfall or ending of your relationship. Without this acknowledgment, you can't grow and reach your higher potential, and will likely repeat the same negative behaviors in a future relationship. Sometimes it takes messing up to do something right.

I know playing the victim may feel safer and allows you to point your finger at your partner, but if you were to strip yourself of this role and examine your own actions, for what could you take responsibility? Retelling your victim story makes you feel powerless. You're likely sharing it from this perspective to try to regain some semblance of control during a chaotic and unmanageable time; but the more you tell it without taking responsibility for your actions, the less control you actually have. I played the victim because it was easier to try to convince my ex that he was making a big mistake, and tell all of my friends that story too, than it was to admit to myself that I was wrong about us. I felt like a failure.

Changing your victim story can also help you shift out of your fiery rage, anxiety, or deep hurt. Author and motivational speaker Gabby Bernstein says, "When you begin to change your stories, you change your experiences. The stories we tell are the experiences we live." Let that powerful statement sink in—"The stories we tell are the experiences we live." The last thing you want to do is relive this story from a victim mentality. When you shift from a victim mind-set and change your breakup narrative, or bigger-picture narrative about love and replace it with a more positive or hopeful message, you can shift your experiences. For instance, "this breakup is the worst thing that ever happened to me" can be shifted to "this breakup is the best thing that ever happened to me." Or, "no one will love me" to "there's an abundance of love out there for me."

ATTACHMENT STYLES

If you still can't put your finger on exactly what went wrong, one major underlying reason that can be hard to articulate is differing levels of comfort and of desire for intimacy. To understand your needs for intimacy, we need to dive into the concepts of *Attachment Theory*. Throughout our life experiences, we have learned that people can be reliable or unreliable, trustworthy or untrustworthy, loving or cruel. The beliefs you have about yourself and others depend on the type of experiences you've had in different relationships. Will someone protect you or hurt you? Will someone be safe and dependable, or harmful and inconsistent? Depending on how people close to you have behaved in the past, you may have very different answers to these questions.

One major influence on the way we feel about ourselves and on our beliefs about how other people will treat us is the interactions we had in childhood with our caregivers. *Attachment Theory* says we form different styles of attachments based on our earliest relationships, which then consciously or unconsciously impact who we choose to date and our behaviors in our adult romantic relationships. Think of your attachment system as how you process the availability and emotional safety of your partner. Not all research supports that our early caregiver interactions are solely responsible for our dysfunctional romantic dynamics. So before you label all your problems as #daddyissues, be aware that a newer review of the existing research by the NIH also suggests that we might be genetically predisposed to have a certain attachment style, since specific genes play a role in social behavior, emotions, and pair bonding. Attachment styles don't come from a single source.

Below I'm going to break down the types of caregiver interactions that have been associated with the three different attachment styles, and the resulting types of adult behaviors. It doesn't take years of psychoanalysis to be able to recognize your type. Notice what comes up for you as you read through the descriptions. For a much more in-depth look at attachment styles, I highly recommend reading *Attached* by Dr. Amir Levine and Rachel Heller. If everyone was required to read this book, I think we'd all have healthier, happier partnerships, with more secure attachments.

Secure Attachment: Your caregiver(s) were sensitive, responsive, kind, respectful, communicative, and affectionate. They consistently provided care when you cried out for help, but also gave you space to be independent and explore the world. You knew if you needed them, they'd be there to support you and guide you. They were good role models of unconditional love. As an adult, you are confident, resilient, and get along well with others. Secure attachments produce very steady, stable relationships full of closeness, communication, trust, and reliability on a partner. You expect your partners to also be loving and responsive to your needs and to treat you with dignity and respect. You welcome intimacy and closeness, and you communicate easily about relationship issues. You're sensitive to your partner's needs, you can compromise, and you're able to be vulnerable. You easily see yourself in a healthy, long-term relationship. You tend to lose interest in evasive people who are inconsistent because you don't play games, and you attribute their inability to communicate as indicative of their behavior rather than as a reflection of your own flaws or that you did something wrong.

A good example of secure attachment is my client Stephanie. Stephanie grew up in a tight-knit family, who had dinner together every night, and her parents were involved in her extracurricular activities. Steph had difficulty dating in college because she was thrown off by the lack of commitment and hookup culture, which she had never experienced in high school where she dated the same guy for three years. When she came into my office, she'd been in a committed relationship with Luke for the past two years, but was questioning if he was really the right person for her. Luke wanted to move in together, but she wasn't ready for that step. Steph said she loved Luke and thought the majority of their relationship was great, but was concerned that he didn't value family in the same way she did. His cynical attitude could get under her skin and ruin her bubbly moods. She worried that breaking up with Luke was a mistake because she'd be throwing a good fish back into the sea. After working through her conflicting feelings, Steph decided to call it quits. Although sad, she generally felt relieved and approached dating confidently since she believed there were good men out there. Within the year she began spending time with an old acquaintance from college. She appreciated his similar passion for family and his positive attitude, and they quickly fell in love. They moved in together and got married two summers later.

Anxious Attachment: Your caregiver(s) were inconsistent in their care for you for various reasons, such as they were busy working in their careers, had mental health or substance use issues, struggled with poverty, or were dealing with an abusive partner. Sometimes they were nurturing, other times intrusive or insensitive, so you learned to be persistent and clingy, knowing your needs would eventually be met. Over the years you may have sought attention by acting out, or by excelling in things like academics and sports in hopes of praise, validation, and affection. As an adult you thrive in some areas, but you struggle with emotional intimacy, craving a lot of closeness mixed with feelings of unworthiness. You fear that you're not enough or worry that you're unlovable. In your romantic relationships, you're often looking to find a partner who can complete you and give you lots of attention. You're needy and insecure, and can come off as desperate when you feel your partner pulling away. You may struggle to tell your partner what you really want because you don't want to accidentally push them away, or come across as "too much." You're fearful of rejection. You need a lot of reassurance and question your partner's feelings and commitment. You tend to get attached very quickly. Brain research done using MRI imaging (which tracks brain activity through blood flow) supports that women with an anxious attachment style react more strongly to negative relationship scenarios, such as conflict, breakups, or death of partner, and are less able to regulate their emotions. Basically, these women get more worked up, and have a harder time self-soothing. They also can pick up on people's emotions more quickly, which means they are more sensitive to detecting when someone is pulling away. Because you struggle to regulate your emotions, dating can be extrastressful. For example, if someone hasn't called or texted when they said they would, you feel on edge until you hear from them.

My client Jamie is an example of an anxious attachment background. She grew up with multiple nannies because both of her parents were high-powered attorneys and spent much of their time working. Jamie remembers having a different nanny almost every year, so she got used to adjusting quickly to having someone new in her life. Jamie always put a lot of pressure on herself to perform well in school in hopes of winning her parents' approval, and remembers feeling the only time her dad was really proud of her was when she got a scholarship to play field hockey in college. In terms of her love life, Jamie identified a pattern of falling hard for emotionally unavailable men and entering relationships that would often end dramatically. These relationships tended to be followed by a multi-month relationship with guys she described as "safe" and "self-esteem boosters." Jamie reports once her confidence was back, the safe men would seem boring, so she'd break up with them. In the more unstable relationships, Jamie would compromise a lot, avoid conflict, and seek out validation, behaving in ways that gave her partner all the power. She never quite felt like herself, and was typically on edge in these relationships. She thought if she didn't press too hard for commitment, these guys would eventually want to wife her up.

What Jamie learned in our dating coaching sessions is that this roller coaster of emotions is not actually love, but rather an activated anxious attachment system. The highs and lows, insecurity, drama, and passion of dating avoidant men (who she didn't recognize at the time were avoidant) kept her guessing and pursuing relationships that didn't meet her needs. Dr. Levine sums it up perfectly in *Attached*: "You start to equate the anxiety, the preoccupation, the obsession, and those ever-so-short bursts of joy with love. What you're really doing is equating an activated attachment system with passion." Jamie now knows some of those safe guys from her past were actually men with secure attachment styles, who would have treated her like a princess had she been able to receive the love she desired. However, at the time she wasn't ready because she didn't truly believe she deserved it due to her underlying feelings of unworthiness from childhood.

Avoidant Attachment: Your caregiver(s) likely did not respond when you were distressed or hurt, and due to their emotional unavailability, you learned how to be independent and take care of your own needs. You didn't receive much affection or attention, and you could have been the victim of neglect or emotional, physical, or sexual abuse. As an adult, you're self-reliant and enjoy having your own space. In your romantic relationships, you are distant and withdraw both physically and emotionally when you feel like your partner wants too much. You tend to either shut down or explode in an argument, and have difficulty expressing your emotions and discussing relationship issues. Your partner may wonder where the relationship is heading and feel left in the dark. You do want love, but you value your independence, so you commonly find yourself in a push-and-pull dynamic. You tend to belittle and criticize your partner to keep them at a distance. and idealize what a relationship *should* be, which prevents you from ever getting too invested in someone since you haven't found the "perfect" person.

A prime avoidant example is my client Tessa, who came from a divorced home. She doesn't remember her father, who left when she was a child, and her mom struggled with depression and alcoholism. As a child, Tessa recalls there was often drama in the home and remembers feeling embarrassed at having to ask her teacher for lunch money because her mom sent her to school empty-handed. At two different points in her childhood the department of child and family services was involved in her care. Tessa said her mom had a string of boyfriends and that when they were in the picture she never felt like a priority. As an adult, Tessa has low self-esteem, and struggled to form healthy relationships due to a hard time opening up and trusting. Tessa reports she briefly dated someone she considered a good guy, but he ended things because she wasn't physically affectionate enough. Tessa says she often feels torn between wanting a committed partner and doing things on her own so she doesn't have to rely on anyone. Ultimately she does want a family, and she's worried she won't be able to keep a relationship long enough to make it all happen. Much of our work together focused on helping Tessa learn the skills, mind-set, and behavior to shift into a more secure attachment. I'm happy to write that while this book was being edited, Tessa connected with someone online, they've been exclusively dating for a few months, met each other's families, and she thinks he's a keeper!

EXERCISE: FIGURING OUT MY ATTACHMENT STYLE

Think about the relationship with your ex and review the statements below, marking each one as *true* or *false*.

Group 1

1. I tell my partner what's on my mind.

2. It's easy for me to get close to my partner.

3. Being affectionate with my partner comes naturally.

4. It's easy to ask my partner for what I want and need in our relationship.

5. When we argue, I don't question if this is the right relationship for me.

6. I feel confident in giving and receiving love.

7. I trust my partner.

Group 2

1. I worry that my partner doesn't really love me.

2. My partner is never as close as I want them to be.

3. I like to stir up drama or play games to know that my partner cares.

4. I'm afraid my partner will leave me, especially if they get to know the real me.

5. I often doubt myself in the relationship.

6. I worry that when I'm not around, my partner may leave me for someone else.

7. When I'm not in a relationship, I feel on edge or incomplete.

Group 3

1. I prefer not to show my partner how I really feel.

2. I like to solve relationship problems on my own.

3. Sometimes I put my partner down or push them away and don't know why.

4. My partner wants me to be closer than I feel comfortable being.

5. During conflict with my partner, I tend to shut down or explode.

6. I struggle to show my partner the attention and affection they need.

7. I don't like depending on my partner.

Add up your true statements for Group 1: _____
Add up your true statements for Group 2: _____
Add up your true statements for Group 3: _____

Group 1 represents a secure attachment, group 2 represents an anxious attachment, and group 3 represents an avoidant attachment. Labeling a statement as true corresponds with having characteristics of that style.

In general, think of a secure style as being comfortable with closeness and intimacy, feeling confident in your relationship, and not stressing about your partner's feelings for you. For an anxious style, think of it as really wanting a lot of intimacy and closeness, but worrying about where the relationship is heading and your partner's feelings for you. Broadly, in an avoidant style you often feel overwhelmed with a lot of intimacy, and you seem to care more about your independence than the relationship. Now that you can identify your own style, which type was your ex?

If your type is predominantly anxious or avoidant, it can be challenging to pick a healthy partner. In fact, some longitudinal studies and existing research suggest people with avoidant and anxious attachments are drawn to each other because they validate each other's framework. The anxious partner comes off needy and insecure and worries they will be left, and the avoidant person views the anxious partner as depending too much on the relationship and pushes them away. The avoidant person is reaffirmed that romantic partners will encroach upon their freedom and despite wanting love they are better off alone, and the anxious person is reminded that partners will push away their love and reject their attempts for connection. An anxious person may dismiss dating a secure person early on because they aren't used to someone being so straightforward with their affection and pursuits. Because they are used to the push and pull, the anxious person may feel it's not enough of a challenge, and push the secure person away thinking it's a chemistry issue. Couples in which both partners are avoidant don't tend to work out because neither is committal and consistent enough to make the relationship work, and a secure person may become frustrated with the emotional distance of a partner with an avoidant attachment. Yet, the anxious and avoidant singles are drawn together magnetically into a turbulent relationship because it feels comfortable and familiar to each individual due to their early life experiences of relating to others.

You likely experienced these feelings since childhood, and this breakup only exacerbates what you falsely believe to be true about love. You may wind up unconsciously choosing partners who feel familiar and exhibit some of the same negative qualities or behaviors as your parents, or past partners. Unconsciously, it feels like you're trying to heal old wounds and fight the same fights in every relationship. You could wind up picking a partner with whom you keep trying to solve these unresolved issues over and over again. This is where working with a therapist or coach can be extremely helpful. Every negative experience only perpetuates your dysfunctional thoughts, leading to false statements and internalized beliefs, such as "all men are bad," "everyone will hurt me," or "I'm unlovable." In reality, you just need to process and understand these past hurts and ideally find a more secure partner. By dating someone secure, it will help *you* become more secure.

Attachment styles also play a role in how you react to your breakup. Research shows those higher in anxious attachments were more sensitive to rejection, had lower levels of self-esteem, and experienced the most adverse effects of a breakup. This makes sense because those with an anxious attachment depend more heavily on having a partner meet their needs and struggle to regulate their emotions, especially in comparison to those with an avoidant attachment, who are more independent and less emotional. Regardless of your attachment style, breakups can wound everyone.

The beautiful thing about love and relationships is that you're not doomed to fail, even if you had crappy caregivers. It's possible to create a secure attachment with any of your partners; it just requires you to understand your past experiences so that you can build a stronger, more secure attachment. In Dr. Stan Tatkin's book *Wired for Love,* he discusses one of my favorite concepts, the *couple bubble*—go on, say that three times fast! Tatkin describes a couple bubble as a "mutually constructed membrane, cocoon, or womb that holds a couple together and protects each partner from outside elements." This bubble is created when you operate from a strong, secure base. This means committing to protecting and prioritizing each other, taking responsibility to voice your needs and trusting your partner will do their best to meet them, turning toward your partner instead of away during times of conflict, and taking action to repair any hurts quickly with effective communication. You approach issues as a team, no matter who is at fault. You both proactively safeguard your relationship from infidelity by setting appropriate boundaries at all times. There's no push and pull, distancing strategies, or games being played in the couple bubble. Keep this in mind for your future relationships.

How did attachment styles come into play and keep intimacy at bay in your relationship that ended? Understanding how your early childhood experiences play into your adult romantic relationships is essential in taking steps to becoming a more securely attached partner in your next relationship. Without even having to change your attachment style, just being aware of how these three types relate can help you choose smarter and better communicate your needs in a relationship. Keep reading to learn about how I shifted from anxious to secure to create a relationship in which I feel adored instead of unworthy.

CHAPTER 8

Reframe Your Breakup— Pain into Wisdom Gained

I wanted really clear reasons for my own big breakup. My ex told me that I just wasn't the one he saw himself marrying. I couldn't grasp this. How could he date me for so long if I wasn't The One? Why couldn't he clearly articulate his concerns during one of the many conversations we had about our future together? I thought this whole "It's just a feeling" was nonsense, and instead of accepting that we weren't the best fit, I internalized it as though I was inherently flawed. What I know now was that "feeling" was his gut—a self-protective response—his own inner voice telling him something was off. Occasionally concrete reasons don't exist, but more often people are not insightful enough or lack the emotional language to dig deep and identify them. Sometimes it will become clearer to them once they've dated other people and have clarity about what exactly was missing in their relationship with you. Many times, the issues are related to attachment styles, misaligned core values, conflicting personality traits, or someone not being able to prioritize the relationship at that time in their life. Only when I started dating other people and met my ideal match was I finally able to put my finger on exactly what my ex was never able to articulate as a deal breaker.

Ultimately, we were both trying to compromise on our core values, which you should *never* do. We talked about our different views on religion and how this would impact raising children, but we never labeled them as a deal breaker because that felt so far in the future. I described my wishes for how I wanted to raise these hypothetical kids and my expectations for the holidays. At times I could tell he was uncomfortable with these discussions, but he never said, "You know what, Sam, I'm really concerned about this because it goes against my belief system and because I'm not comfortable with this; I think we need to sit down and talk about whether we should build a future together." We also had different approaches to spending and saving money, which is a hot topic that frequently brings couples into my therapy office. It bothered me that he made a big deal of spending money to go out to restaurants or on travel, and it annoyed him that I'd do retail therapy at T.J.Maxx and bring home non-necessities. We valued spending money on different things, and some of this is rooted in our differing socioeconomic backgrounds and the messages we received about money growing up. He wanted to live in the country, and I preferred to live in the suburbs, with the ability to escape to the wilderness. We also came from different upbringings, his as an only child in a twice-divorced household and mine with a sibling and happily married parents, which impacted our beliefs about love, marriage, and family.

Though much of our relationship was positive and we had mutual interests, we blissfully ignored the weight of our misaligned core values for so long because we were young and in love. Were you blinded by love too? The biggest gift you can give yourself is to get clear on your core values, which we'll dive into later in the book. Eventually, these differing values became some of the major deal breakers that caused him to end our relationship; he just wasn't able to articulate this at the time and I wasn't ready to own these things as deal breakers. Truth be told, I was always worried about these issues, but I stuffed the concerns down and naively thought with love and commitment we could work through them. I also felt shame and embarrassment to admit I had invested my time and energy into someone that wasn't my best match, so I felt this powerful drive to force it to work. The more love, commitment, finances, and time you've invested into a relationship, the harder it is to break up. I wish my older, wiser self could have told me never to compromise on what's most important, and that change and starting over could actually be a very positive experience. In the right relationship, you'll maintain a healthy sense of self, and your core values will be honored and shared.

Our love languages also differed, and frankly he couldn't figure out how to speak mine. You may have heard the term "love languages" before, which was coined by Dr. Gary Chapman in his book *The Five Love Languages*. The gist of this concept is that we each have a primary and secondary love language, which is the most meaningful way in which we like to receive love. We don't necessarily show love in the way that we like to receive it. Disconnection and conflict can arise for couples when they don't feel like their partner is showing them the type of love they most desire. There is no right or wrong love language, which is why it's so important to understand each one and figure out what impacts your partner the most. The five love languages, in no particular order, are:

Words of Affirmation: The use of words to affirm your partner, whether through love letters or by verbally telling your partner how much he or she means to you. Your partner values being praised, adored, and loved through words, letters, texts, or public displays, such as a thoughtful Facebook post.

Acts of Service: Actions speak louder than words in this love language, so showing love through helping out around the house, child-rearing, and running errands goes a long way. If you can take stress off your partner's shoulders, this makes them feel very cared for.

Physical Touch: Showing your love through physical affection, which can be sex, but also includes hugs, kisses, holding hands, massages, and other forms of intimate physical contact.

Gifts: Giving a thoughtful gift makes your partner feel most loved. Many times it's the thought behind the gift that counts, and less about the material good itself.

Quality Time: Giving your partner your undivided attention and spending time together. Sometimes it doesn't matter what activity you're doing, as long as you're present and tuned into your partner without distractions.

EXERCISE: LOVE LANGUAGES

Go online and take the free love language quiz (http://www.5lovelanguages.com/profile), then write down your corresponding scores for each of the five categories in your Bounce Back Journal for easy reference.

- ♥ Were you surprised by your primary love language, or by the scores in each category?

- ♥ On a scale from 1 to 10 (1 = no effort, 5 = occasional effort, 10 = daily effort), in your opinion how much effort did your ex put into speaking your love language(s)? On the same scale, how much effort did you put into speaking their love language?

- ♥ Describe specific examples or situations in which your ex spoke your love language(s).

- ♥ Describe specific examples or situations in which your ex struggled to speak your love language(s) or did not make you feel loved.

- ♥ In what ways do you think you could have more clearly communicated or asked your ex to speak your love language(s)?

- ♥ What are some concrete actions or ways in which a future partner can speak your love language(s) and make you feel loved?

My ex spoke to me through physical touch, often snuggling in bed before going to sleep, but I remember wanting more daily hugs and kisses once the honeymoon phase wore off. We'd also spend quality time together hiking and camping on the weekends, which are some of my happiest memories from the relationship. However, I often felt he only wanted to spend this quality time doing the activities he enjoyed, and would moan and groan when I'd ask to stop at a crafts fair, go shopping, or eat out. I definitely craved more words of affirmation than he'd give me, wanting to hear more declarative statements of love, compliments, and praise. Looking back on it,

I even remember asking for gifts, which is definitely *not* my top love language. I wanted to know I was on his mind and that he'd go out of his way to do something thoughtful. I remember one time being in tears, asking him to spontaneously bring home flowers—telling him concretely what would make me feel more loved. Never happened, and don't even get me started about my grad school graduation when he had to work late and didn't make time to pick up a bouquet. My *dad* did it and they pretended it was from my boyfriend (shout-out to my father for always being there for me). At the time I couldn't figure out how I could get him to love me more and *want* to do these things. I couldn't change his resistant attitude. I thought there was something wrong with me and that if I was fun enough, or flexible enough, or less needy, he'd step up and meet my needs. I couldn't see it was his own avoidant issues. The more I wanted to be loved, the more he'd pull away.

My biggest conclusion about why we broke up is due to differing needs and desires for intimacy. My ex had an avoidant attachment style, which conflicted with my desire for closeness and for us to function as a unit. He liked to assert his independence and did things consciously and unconsciously to push me away. Basically, I had a "we factor" and he had a "me factor." For instance, one year he wanted to go skiing on his holiday break at home in the mountains and because I couldn't keep up on the slopes, instead of telling me his concern he said, "You're not family" as his reason for not wanting me to travel home with him, instantly wounding me and keeping me at a distance. Or the time we argued because he didn't want to invite me to his holiday office party, saying that sometimes I don't have a filter and he didn't want to be embarrassed by me. In classic avoidant fashion, he liked to belittle and poke fun at me, saying that he wished I was smarter, stating, "What you don't know could fill a warehouse!" Or, when driving around in his truck I'd sing in my typical off-key tone, horrendously and hilariously misquoting lyrics. He'd smack my leg, annoyed, and demand that I stop. I'd laugh, downplay or normalize these behaviors, thinking to myself *gosh my singing voice must be really bad*, never stopping to question that if he loved me why would he treat me disrespectfully. What I didn't know then was that these types of distancing behaviors are common for someone with an avoidant attachment style. In contrast, when my husband entered my life, it was so refreshing to find someone so positive and secure who rocks out to the air guitar with me while I belt out the wrong lyrics and sing at the top of my lungs, who couldn't wait to introduce me to his professional networks, and who genuinely thinks I'm the greatest person in the world.

As I was writing this book, my ex generously agreed to take an attachment style assessment available in the book *Attached* so that I could more concretely illustrate for you some of the interpersonal behaviors I experienced. I will say, in his defense, he's been very supportive of my writing this book, and we've been able to cultivate a respectful, platonic friendship. I can now look back on our relationship with both positive and negative memories, but generally I have a warm regard for him, rather than the hurt and anger that initially colored the entire relationship during the breakup. His responses to the assessment confirmed all that I had experienced, and it was quite validating—nothing was wrong with me. I wasn't flawed, and the breakup didn't have to do with me not loving him enough. He scored a 10 out of 14 on the avoidant scale, a 6 of 14 on the secure scale, and a 5 of 14 on the anxious scale. Below are some examples of the avoidant emotions and behaviors he displayed throughout the course of our relationship:

- ♥ He didn't feel comfortable relying and depending on me
- ♥ He preferred not to share his innermost feelings
- ♥ His independence was more important to him than our relationship
- ♥ He had great difficulty expressing his needs and wants
- ♥ He sometimes felt angry or annoyed with me without knowing why
- ♥ It made him nervous when I got too close
- ♥ In our relationship, he wasn't sure what he wanted anymore

These avoidant thoughts and behaviors led to an underlying feeling in the relationship that I consistently wanted more than he could give me, and that when I wanted the comfort of emotional intimacy he sometimes pulled away, making me feel not good enough. Reflecting on my past romantic experiences, I could see a pattern in which since middle school I gave everything I had to make it work with my boyfriends (or guys I had crushes on that refused to call me their girlfriend), but I often settled for far less than I deserved. It wasn't until I met my husband that I found a partner who was equally reliable, and I felt confident trusting. I truly loved myself in this relationship, and could ease into a more secure attachment.

So you can fully grasp how much you can transform, and that there's an even better love for you on the other side of your breakup, I want to tell you the rest of my love story. I sent the first message online, and he responded that, "As beautiful as your smile is, I'm actually online right now to deactivate my account. I met someone and we're going to give it a shot, but please send me your email so I can reach out if things don't work out." My heart sank a little, but I appreciated his honesty and I liked that he was looking for a commitment. Fast forward a few weeks, to my surprise, there he was in my e-mail inbox saying things didn't work out, and that he remembered me, my profile, and the red dress I was wearing in my photo! After a couple emails back and forth, and a fantastic phone call, I found myself eating sushi, laughing, and listening to this handsome hunk talk about his interests, like volunteering as a high school basketball coach because he finds it rewarding to help boys grow into more confident, accountable men (yes, these men do exist!). The date went so well that we grabbed an after-dinner drink, and then I found myself tossing on sneakers with my dress so we could shoot hoops together at a nearby park.

To my surprise, he texted the next day, and called the following day to ask me on a second date. I was so used to anxiously waiting by my phone, that I was confused when he reached out so quickly. The perks of dating someone with a secure attachment are that you always know where you stand. We went out again two days later, and I want to say the rest is history, but I was only three months out of my soul-crushing breakup, my heart was still bleeding. I needed more time to heal myself, and to date around to get crystal clear on what it was that I was searching for. We casually dated and continued to get to know each other. With every date and call, we grew closer and I could see major potential, but what's messed up is that I thought something might be wrong with him because it felt *too* easy.

You see, I was used to dating *boys*. Ya know, *bad boys*. I loved the thrill of the chase, and assumed the intensity and angst of not knowing if I'd get that coveted GF status was just part of falling in love. I was used to dating guys who didn't prioritize me, couldn't communicate clearly about their feelings, and who weren't emotionally available—all warning signs of an avoidant attachment. I'd get just enough validation that someone had feelings for me, so I'd cling to that glimmer of hope, but I mostly felt anxious and insecure until I heard from them again. Deep down I knew my husband had the qualities of a man I wanted to marry, but I misread my own calm and ease as a sign I might not be interested. I was lacking the "excitement" (aka anxiety) I'd grown accustomed to. Where were all of the ups and downs in this relationship? I may have created a bit of drama and almost pushed him to the point of no return when my ex contacted me and tried to come back into the picture. But, this time I wasn't going to let my anxious attachment style rear its ugly head and keep me from giving the best man I ever met a real chance. I was over these games, and ready to get off the emotional roller coaster. Real love is passionate, but it's also easy, safe, and consistent. You're never left in the dark, you have a teammate, and it feels balanced. I had an aha moment, where I literally said out loud to myself, "Sam, what are you doing?" I was keeping an incredible, high-quality man at a distance. I had a deep moment of clarity that I will remember forever. I said to myself, *You deserve this fairy-tale type of love. Accept the love that you've always wanted.* And after that? My love journey quickly unfolded with a man who became my best friend for life.

He was consistent in his communication and pursuit of me, a true characteristic of someone with a secure attachment. In four months of dating, he saw and understood all of me, more than my ex of four years ever had, and he spoke all of the love languages. I don't like when people say relationships take work. When you pick the right partner, they require ongoing *effort*, but *work* makes it sound arduous. When you're with your ideal match you want to put in the effort because your partner makes you happy. When both partners equally invest energy into each other and show up vulnerably and authentically, they can create a rewarding and meaningful relationship. It will feel especially easy and synchronized when you both have secure attachments. I'm not saying you can't make it work if you have conflicting attachment styles; it will just feel like work because you'll be managing a lot of conflict around not feeling as loved and adored as you want to be.

I like to say I'm very grateful—my heart is bursting with gratitude—for my current love life, but not lucky. Luck implies it happened by chance, but I intentionally created the life that I'm living. I got out of my own way, upped my standards for myself, and opened myself up to receive the love that I believed I deserved. I thoroughly processed my breakup, learned from my love lessons, put effort into my own self-care, and prioritize my relationship every single day. It's not something I can have and you can't, which is why I'm so thrilled that you're investing in yourself right now by reading this book. Now it's up to you to take action.

TURNING YOUR BREAKUP BAGGAGE INTO LOVE LESSONS

Even though you're still in pain, by evaluating the dynamics of your old relationship you're already taking steps on your new love journey. Let that sink in. The way you wrap up this relationship with your ex will directly impact the next person you welcome into your life. Many women feel stuck and trapped in the time between relationships—like they're not moving forward, that this "in-between" period is a waste of time, and ultimately that a relationship status defines them. What's even worse is that they sit and wait for time to heal their broken heart, without doing any work themselves, and then unconsciously bring baggage into their next relationship, only to feel unfulfilled or break up due to similar circumstances. Healing requires active effort. By gaining more insight and understanding around your heartbreak, and taking steps to heal and reflect, you're actively laying a solid foundation on which to build a new epic love story. The best part is you don't have to do it alone. The objective perspective and feedback provided when working with a therapist or coach can help you recognize your patterns and more thoroughly explore your attachment style. With this greater awareness, you heal not only from this breakup, but from past hurts, and you'll be better prepared to seek out a more secure partner in the future.

People have a tendency to ask themselves if they were good enough. You can exchange any word for "good"—smart, pretty, fun, skinny, outgoing, patient, spontaneous, generous, etc. You know what I have to say? *Enough* of that! Tell yourself you are enough. Right now. Say it out loud. "I am enough." I couldn't hear you, say it again! A relationship is not a trial where one person has to measure up to the other. It's more like a puzzle where the pieces have to fit. Your relationship may have had the potential to be a perfect puzzle, but all of the pieces didn't align. Stop trying to glue the broken puzzle that is your relationship back together. Puzzle pieces can be a very close fit—initially, the shape looks right, but when you try to put the tab into the slot, you realize it simply doesn't align. You can try to jam it into place (change yourself or try to change them), but ultimately it's not the right piece. You may realize that you were the piece constantly trying to fit into their puzzle, rather than each of you being pieces that come together to create one puzzle. You should each be pieces with equal weight, creating an extraordinary puzzle together.

Do not, I repeat, *do not*, change your core values or things that you admire about yourself in an attempt to win your ex back. This won't make you happy and only leads to resentment. The changes you make should be based on what you, a confident, worthy, self-loving woman values. This can take some time to figure out. It's natural in a close relationship to take on each other's hobbies, interests, traits, and perspectives, which enable you to grow and change. Self-evolution is an ingredient for happiness. One of the rewarding things about being in a relationship is this expansion of knowledge and self-concept, which is the compilation of your attributes, beliefs, preferences, and attitudes. When you're in a relationship you learn, grow, expand your worldview, and take on new hobbies that are influenced by your partner. Your self-concept and how you view yourself broadens and develops. Yet this can also exacerbate and increase the pain of a breakup, since the loss of your partner also feels like the loss of yourself.

In a study called "Who Am I Without You? The Influence of Romantic Breakup on the Self-Concept," lead researcher Erica Slotter and her colleagues examined how overlapping self-concepts leave individuals' self-concepts vulnerable to change when the relationship ends, and found that participants had reduced self-concept clarity after a breakup. Basically, they didn't know who they were anymore, which also predicted emotional distress postbreakup. The more we grow as a person when in the relationship, the more lost and uncertain we feel of who we are after the relationship. That's because we've allowed our partner to rub off on us, and when we lose them, we question what parts are us, what parts are them and whether we need to "return" those borrowed parts, or keep them and be forever changed.

Researchers Lauren Howe and Carol Dweck have conducted some innovative breakup studies to learn why some people are haunted by their romantic past and others seem to move on with minimal difficulty. In one study, they asked participants to reflect on a time they were rejected, and asked them to respond to the question, "What did you take away from this rejection?" They found that some people drew weak connections between rejection and the self, attributing the rejection to an arbitrary force rather than a personal flaw, such as, "I learned that two people can both be quality individuals, but that doesn't mean they belong together." Others allowed the rejection to define them. These participants submitted responses such as, "I learned that I am too sensitive and that I push people away to avoid them pushing me away first. This characteristic is negative and makes people crazy and drives them away." Howe writes in *The Atlantic*, "In these types of stories, rejection uncovered a hidden flaw, one that led people to question or change their own views of themselves—and, often, they portrayed their personalities as toxic, with negative qualities likely to contaminate other relationships." In their research, participants reported the most prolonged distress after a rejection caused them to question who they really were and caused their self-image to change for the worse. In other words, if the rejection seemed to reveal a negative truth about a person, it became a heavier and more painful burden. Howe writes, "When rejection is intimately linked to self-concept, people are also more likely to experience a fear of it. People reported becoming more guarded with new partners and 'putting up walls' . . . The belief that rejection revealed a flaw prompted people to worry that this defect would resurface in other relationships. They worried that future relationships would continue to fail, voicing fears that no matter how hard they tried, they would not be able to find someone new to love them."

You can probably see how attachment styles and long-standing emotional injuries come into play here. Howe and Dweck conclude that separating rejection from the self, and the stories you tell yourself about rejection, can make your breakup easier. Assuming you're inherently flawed is the most damaging thing you can do. It's a sure way to stay stuck in this breakup grief. Rather than blame yourself, externalize the breakup to differing needs— whether it's different core values, personalities, or desires for intimacy. Instead of feeling that you're not enough or unworthy, validate your own needs and desires, and reframe your negative self-concept into something positive, such as "I am enough, and we just weren't right for each other." You have time in this journey for growth, to heal wounds, and to reframe your "flaws" into gifts that allow you to live more authentically and embrace vulnerability.

Understanding the reasons behind your breakup is really a personal growth experience that'll transform you into a more insightful and woke version of yourself. These are your love lessons—the most valuable takeaways from your heartbreak. Let's now do a reflective exercise in which you identify your love lessons learned, which will increase your self-awareness and help you pick an ideal match in the future.

EXERCISE: LOVE LESSONS LEARNED

- ♥ How did I use this relationship to try to heal emotional injuries from childhood?

- ♥ In what ways did this breakup validate my internalized beliefs about myself, how others will treat me, and about love?

- ♥ What did I like about myself in this relationship? What positive feelings, behaviors, and qualities did it bring out in me?

- ♥ What did I not like about myself in this relationship? What negative feelings, behaviors, and qualities did it bring out in me?

- ♥ What qualities did I like and admire about my ex?

- ♥ What qualities did I not like about my ex?

- ♥ How did I feel loved by my ex?

- ♥ How did I not feel loved by my ex?

- ♥ My ex did a good job providing . . .

- ♥ My ex did a poor job providing . . .

- ♥ My relationship was lacking . . .

- ♥ I liked myself most in our relationship when . . .

- ♥ I liked myself least in our relationship when . . .

- ♥ How was I not honoring my needs and desires in this relationship?
- ♥ From this experience, I learned that I absolutely must have . . .
- ♥ In the future I will compromise on . . .
- ♥ In the future, I will never compromise (aka deal breakers) on . . .
- ♥ It's important that my future partner appreciates my . . .
- ♥ I will not settle for . . .

In every romantic experience, whether it's just one date or a short-lived fling, you're collecting *dating data*. Your dating data is what informs your love lessons. And unlike one of my previous clients from the Massachusetts Institute of Technology, who mapped out all of her dating data on Excel, looking for data points and trying to create algorithms to draw conclusions, you don't have to be a math whiz to walk away with some key love lessons! Dating data is information about what makes you want to run the other way, and what qualities, values, traits, and behaviors qualify someone as an ideal match. All of this dating data will allow you to become more aware of your negative patterns, challenge your destructive assumptions, and help you start behaving in ways that honor your value and desire to be loved. You can use what you learn to more quickly weed out dating duds and more easily recognize your ideal match when you meet them. Just because you have different opinions, lifestyles, or values from someone doesn't make them a dating dud. A dating dud is someone who's just in it for a hookup, who's emotionally unavailable, or who can't show up authentically and vulnerably. You're ultimately in a better position to find a loving partner because you can use the knowledge you've gained from this breakup to your advantage. See, I told you this wasn't a huge failure!

In order to move in a positive direction, you must *reframe your pain into wisdom gained*. Some of what you learned from your love lessons will dig into old wounds that need to be healed. During this process you should challenge your negative beliefs about love and your own worth. Begin to treat yourself in a way that sets the standards for how others can love you more fully, which means not tolerating BS behaviors and modeling a more secure attachment.

Some people see scars,
and it is wounding
they remember. To me,
they are proof of the fact
that there is healing.

LINDA HOGAN

There are partners out there who will accept all of you, where you won't have to jump through hoops or diminish your wants and needs to receive the love you desire.

Look inwards at yourself instead of outwards at your ex to identify patterns and feelings you've likely experienced your entire life. Sigmund Freud coined the term *repetition compulsion* to describe how a person tends to repeat a traumatic event or patterns of behavior that caused distress early in life. The devastation of your breakup is compounded by other experiences of hurt, rejection, and aloneness, typically inflicted in infancy or childhood by a caretaker who didn't stop to correct his or her neglectful, avoidant, or anxious behavior. Your caregiver probably didn't take the time to explain your experiences and perceptions, to validate your emotions, or to say how much you matter, belong, and are loved. Your experiences of feeling unloved, unimportant, and as though you can't do anything right led to internalized beliefs about yourself and expectations for the way people will treat you. These negative messages informed your behaviors and interactions with others, leading you to believe that you'll be hurt, that someone will disappoint you, that you'll be abandoned, or that you can't rely on anyone but yourself.

My client Zabrina was proposed to five times, and cheated on every partner she's been with. She came to me in distress after breaking up with yet another man. In exploring her complex family history, I learned that Zabrina was born to young teenage parents and her mom was an orphan who lost her own adoptive mother in a tragic accident when she was only twelve. Zabrina was born a few years later, and her parents married when she was three. Growing up, she felt closer to her father, who was more present physically and emotionally. She felt unloved by her mom, who didn't hug or kiss her, or even say "I love you." In middle school Zabrina was a straight A, competitive dancer, who thought if she could perform well enough, she'd get the attention and adoration she craved from her mother, and continue to make her father proud.

Zabrina's world came crashing down in junior high when her father had an affair and her parents went through a nasty divorce. Both parents remarried within a few years, and her father moved three hours away. Zabrina was devestated. She felt abandoned by her father, and resented having to live with her cold and emotionally unavailable mother. She stopped caring about school and had a "massive identity crisis." She spent most of high school bouncing around from different friends' homes and applied to college on her own without the support of her parents.

Zabrina did a lot of soul-searching and personal growth throughout her twenties. She had a life-changing conversation with her mom when she was twenty-seven, asking her what it was like to be pregnant at age fifteen. It was the first time her mother talked to Zabrina as an adult, sharing her truth that she wanted an abortion or to give the baby up for adoption, but Zabrina's father said no. Her mom said Zabrina's father was the first to hold her when she was born, and that she had no idea how to comfort her child, or what being a mom even looked like, since she'd spent many years in an orphanage. Her mother admitted she didn't bond with Zabrina as a baby, and that even when Zabrina was three years old she still wanted to give her up for adoption because, having been adopted herself, she knew how much love a foster family could give her, and she didn't know how to love Zabrina in the way she deserved. It finally clicked for Zabrina that there wasn't anything wrong with her and she wasn't unworthy of love, but rather it was her mother's own avoidant attachment style that kept her from showing Zabrina the love that she craved. It's been almost a decade since that conversation and Zabrina reports the relationship with her mother has significantly improved. However, Zabrina wasn't able to make the connection from her childhood wounds to her adult romantic relationships.

Zabrina's love life over the years was tumultuous, dating men who wanted to be with her and cheating to push them away. She said, "Boyfriends have always come easily for me. I never spend a lot of time single. Men fall in love with me, but I don't fall in love back. I act like I'm in love though because I want love." In order to navigate her conflicted feelings and avoidant behaviors, I provided a framework in which to view how her childhood wounds come into play in her adult romantic relationships.

Zabrina felt abandoned and rejected by her mother most of her life, which led to her struggling with self-worth and feeling loved. From infancy her mother didn't meet many of her emotional needs, so Zabrina inherently learned that she wasn't worthy of a caring relationship, and felt a deep sense of shame. Then, her stable source of love and belonging was rocked when Zabrina learned that her father cheated and he abandoned the family by moving away. Zabrina internalized that the people you love will leave you. In her romantic relationships, she seeks out protective men who take care of her and proclaim their love, which temporarily feels good to Zabrina, since this was lacking in childhood, but only validates her underlying sense of aloneness and unworthiness because they don't know the real, authentic version of her. Because she's so guarded and fearful of being hurt, she rejects these men first before they can hurt and leave her. Her emotional wall, which kept Zabrina safe in childhood from mom's neglect and dad's abandonment, now blocks intimacy. She goes through the superficial actions and gestures of a romantic relationship, but she's lacking the deeper intimate connection. Just as her mother emotionally shut down and rejected her, she's now doing the same to others by keeping men at an emotional distance and cheating. Zabrina also learned from her father's infidelity to act out and release emotions that assault other people's boundaries, driving the people who are trying to love her away and keeping intimacy at arm's length. She sabotages healthy relationships because they feel incongruent with who she believes she is at her core—an unlovable child. Cheating only adds to Zabrina's underlying sense of shame and unworthiness, validating that she's not good enough for love and affection. She acts out in a way that aligns with her underlying wounds. With a better understanding of how her deep-seated childhood hurts impact her romantic relationships, Zabrina can now approach love in a more vulnerable way that facilitates true connection.

Let's now explore your own wounds and disappointments, which exacerbate your current pain, and figure out how they may be tied to some of the grief you're experiencing in this breakup. When you recognize these emotional injuries, you can start acting and behaving in ways that rewrite your dysfunctional narrative and embrace healthier views about love and belonging. Take out your Bounce Back Journal—we're diving deep because honest self-reflection increases insight, helps you to regain control, and empowers you to create a more fulfilling love life.

EXERCISE: EXPLORING EMOTIONAL INJURIES

1. How have you been wounded in love? Looking back at your childhood, can you identify any disappointments, unmet needs, hurts, or conditions of worth that were placed upon you? In

what ways were you told, overtly or covertly, that you were bad, didn't matter, should be embarrassed for who you are or your mistakes, or that you don't deserve love? These may not be things that you've consciously identified and intellectualized before, so the experiences may come to you first as a feeling, a dark icky one that you've pushed deep down where shame lives. Write down these specific incidents and memories from as early back as you can recall with your caregiver(s).

2. What is the primary assumption or conclusion you've drawn about love and internalized to be true? This is a message such as "I am flawed and undeserving of love," "my love will always be unrequited," "everyone will leave me," "I can't depend on anyone to meet my needs," or "no matter what I do I am never enough." Identify and write down the painful, negative beliefs you've carried with you for years.

3. How were these internalized negative beliefs and emotional injuries validated in your dating and romantic experiences? In which relationships did you feel similarly to that wounded, younger version of yourself? How were your worst fears proven to you over and over again? Write down any moments, big or small, in which your past partners behaved in ways that confirmed your destructive assumptions about love.

4. Are your same old assumptions and conclusions about love and how others will treat you being validated in this breakup? Write down how your ex and recent relationship played out feelings of past hurts and validated your emotional injuries.

5. Now that you looked at externals, it's important as an adult to reflect on the ways you created and contributed to certain painful situations. Taking responsibility will help you to create closure in your breakup, and also to heal past wounds. Is anything that you're projecting onto your partner something for which you can take responsibility? For instance, if you feel

unlovable, how did you push away those that showed you love so that you could validate your own dysfunctional framework? If your partner depended on you too much, how did you behave in ways that made them cling to you and violate your freedom? In your recent relationship, how did you rewound yourself? How did you treat yourself similarly to those who hurt you?

- ♥ In what ways were you cruel, unpleasant, or selfish that could have pushed your partner to respond in the ways that they did?
- ♥ How did you not love, value, and respect yourself?
- ♥ In what ways have you kept your standards low to validate your framework?
- ♥ How did you minimize your own physical and emotional needs?
- ♥ How did you put yourself on the back burner?
- ♥ How did you bottle up thoughts and feelings, and then blame your partner for not knowing how you felt?
- ♥ How did you let yourself be taken advantage of or fail to set healthy boundaries?
- ♥ How did you seek approval instead of authentic connection?
- ♥ How did you people-please and give without receiving?
- ♥ How were you defensive and argumentative?
- ♥ How did you act passively instead of asserting yourself?
- ♥ How did you dismiss or discount your own feelings?
- ♥ How did you allow someone else to dictate how you should be treated?
- ♥ How did you push away love and affection?
- ♥ How were you complacent?

- ♥ How did you compromise on things that were important to you?
- ♥ How did you downplay your positive qualities?
- ♥ How did you keep yourself guarded and avoid your vulnerabilities?
- ♥ How did you deprive yourself of love and real connection?

This deeper understanding of yourself, your motives, and your behaviors in relationships may leave you feeling sick to your stomach, full of remorse and regret or sadness that you've allowed it to go on for so long. It's okay to feel these emotions, and they signal a pivotal point in your breakup recovery—self-forgiveness. Once you have fully grasped how your own actions contributed to the breakup, and the underlying reasons for *why* you behaved in these ways, you can begin to forgive yourself for perpetuating these false assumptions about love.

Be kind and gentle with yourself during some of these realizations. You likely settled for less than you deserved because from a young age you believed you didn't deserve any better. You've allowed these destructive assumptions to rule your love life for long enough. I believe we're all wired for love (nature), but nurture has a way of screwing us up. As an adult, you can now see that these dysfunctional beliefs served the purpose of protecting you and keeping you safe as a child. It was your only way of making sense of the world, and the adults in your life didn't know how to show you love in other ways. But now approaching love from these old frameworks just perpetuates them and keeps you trapped in a recurring pattern. It's important to note that some of these experiences were likely unintentionally inflicted upon you. Your caregiver(s) didn't know how to parent more effectively, and there's a good chance they themselves had been abused or neglected, or struggled with mental illness, narcissism, poverty, or other issues that prevented them from knowing how to show you unconditional love. Unfortunately not everyone had parents who would take a teaching moment when you misbehaved to say, "I always love you, but I don't like your behavior right now." Instead of feeling accepted, you felt shamed and flawed. I'm so sorry for your experiences. Everyone deserves to feel worthy of love and belonging.

The bad news is that you can't change the past, but the good news is that you can course-correct the direction in which you're going. You're no longer a helpless child, and as an adult you can rewrite your life narrative by setting healthier expectations for love. You can break the cycle of how others have treated you, and how you've treated yourself. This may mean learning new skills, such as self-love practices, how to be more assertive, setting boundaries, and communicating more effectively. Again, this is where it's helpful to work with an expert. Right now, I challenge you to commit to this self-growth, to refuse to put up with abusive or neglectful behavior, and to set the standards for how you want others to treat you by honoring and loving yourself in that new adult way. I encourage you to operate from a new framework in which you are enough, your needs matter, you feel comfortable being your authentic self, you command respect, and you're worthy of reciprocal love. This may also mean setting boundaries with the people who don't support your new way of engaging with the world and who keep you feeling small, such as toxic family members, or less than supportive friends. You don't necessarily have to cut them out, but you do need to stop tolerating the way they are treating you. The transition will take conscious effort, but it's possible to use these more empowering beliefs as your new baseline from which to date and operate in this more securely attached world.

This exercise may have given you enough closure so that you're able to lovingly detach from the pain of the breakup, feeling inspired to focus on yourself. For some, however, this new insight may motivate you to reach out to your ex to share what you've learned. This isn't the time for mea culpas and asking for amends. You need to continue to focus on yourself in this process, to take responsibility and ownership for your part in the end of the relationship, and to work toward accepting the outcome. I still recommend waiting *at least* three months (though you may need much more time) before engaging in a conversation with your ex. Of course you're under no obligation to contact them at all, and the insight you're unearthing can be your gift that doesn't need to be shared. Keep reading, there are more insights to come!

CHAPTER 9

Status "Quoples"

Did you blossom early as a couple, and then plateau? Did the thrill of the chase keep you invested? Did your determination to change them override your inner voice? Did you grow apart with separate endeavors, but claim you were on the same page? Did you convince yourself that you were just stuck in a temporary rut? Did you stick it out because it was easier than splitting up? Did you wait for a ring on your finger because it was supposed to be the logical next step? You wait around thinking you'll be happier when you get that ring on your finger. The truth is that the potential you had as a couple likely peaked, but because you're loyal, committed, or afraid of change or to be on your own, you convinced yourself to stay in a stagnant relationship.

I call this type of couple—the ones who stay together because it's comfortable, convenient, and complacent—the *status "quople"* (pronounced as if you joined the word "quo" and "couple"). To maintain the status quo is to keep things the way they presently are. Tony Robbins says that in order to be happy, we need to feel a sense of progress. If you were stuck in a status "quople" relationship, the partnership stopped serving you because you weren't growing and reaching your full potential. The beauty in your breakup is that it's now your opportunity for growth.

Some status "quoples" are in love, or content, but ultimately not growing and evolving. Status "quoples" stay together for multiple reasons, whether

111

because change is scary and no one wants to rock the boat, or because people worry that they won't find anyone better. I was guilty of being part of a status "quople." My justification was that I was in love, dreaded starting over, had already put in so much effort, and was afraid of "failing."

It takes significant introspection and courage to pull back and identify yourself as being part of a status "quople." I want you to question if the relationship served its purpose—not to end up together, but rather to give you the love lessons you need to get back out there and find your more ideal match? Imagine that. How does this change your perception about your breakup?

If your needs went unmet despite clearly communicating your expectations for change, there's a good chance you settled. It can be easier to see it in other couples' relationships, since we tend to be blind in our own love lives, and frankly it can be easier to stick your head in the sand than take action. While with your ex, you may have tried to force a future together, or check off milestones (for example, moving in together, making it to the next anniversary, getting engaged or married) because you wanted a sense of progress, especially if you tend to compare yourself to friends (or frenemies) on social media. It can be hard when everyone around you seems to be growing and taking steps forward in life, and you're stuck or feel like you're falling behind. You probably continued to invest time, energy, love, commitment, and finances into the relationship in an effort to prove yourself right—telling yourself that somehow it was going to work even though deep down it felt off.

You start to question your own judgment. How could you be so "wrong" about your own feelings. After an experience like this, you may have difficulty trusting yourself again, fearful you'll make another bad choice with a new partner. But beating yourself up will only make you doubt your decisions more. Be willing to honestly evaluate where you went wrong in the last relationship, and have faith in your ability to learn from your mistakes.

Many status "quoples" are more in love with the *idea* of their relationship than the reality of it. For example, with my ex, I had a crush on him for so long that I was head over heels when we first got together. But, as time went on and I took off my rose-colored glasses, I began to realize I was still infatuated with the idea of him, but not totally satisfied with who he

The minute you settle
for less than you deserve,
you get even less
than you settled for.

MAUREEN DOWD

actually was and how we worked as a couple. Because of the dramatic build-up of intense initial feelings, I convinced myself that we were meant to be, instead of embracing the reality that we weren't meant for the long haul. A relationship that ends can still be wildly successful and serve a purpose. He was a catch, just not *my* catch.

The mind does funny things to justify our life decisions, especially when we have two potential paths to go down without a clear "right" choice. To stay in or leave the relationship, that's the million-dollar question. We often analyze the pros and cons of each option endlessly before we're forced to make a choice. Because you can probably come up with good reasons for either path, your mind doesn't like the fact that it has to choose only one outcome. This angst is called cognitive dissonance, which is when we have conflicting thoughts, behaviors, or beliefs that make us feel uncomfortable and anxious. In order to relieve this mental discomfort and restore balance, we rationalize and create support for our choices and it makes us feel better and less torn. We tend to justify the status quo because even if we're unhappy with it, it's in our comfort zone. When something is familiar our brain knows we can survive in this state, so we tend to minimize loss to protect our safety. A big breakup is the ultimate loss because it's a survival threat, so you convince yourself to stay. In a twisted way, my thought process was *if I've invested this much, he must be The One; I'll get over the things that don't feel right; he'll change in the future; we'll make it work.* The risk would be to believe and take action on the thought that *there's someone else out there who is a more ideal match and even if I don't know who or where he is, I'm going to leave my current relationship to go find it.* Your loss aversion system is always weighing pros and cons, and because you've already "paid" (i.e., invested emotions, energy, time, and finances), a breakup would cost you too much. You're more inclined to take a risk when you can predict that the pain of your breakup will be offset by the joy of your gain, whether that's living life on your own terms, or finding a more perfect match.

But in the right relationship, both your heart and head will agree; you won't have to choose between them. The decision to stay will be a no-brainer.

When I later fell in love with my husband, it made everything about my breakup blaringly clear. I can be an extremely indecisive person—the type who samples every flavor of ice cream before committing to one scoop. And if you knew how much I love ice cream, you'd understand that I take the order of a delicious cone almost as seriously as that of picking my future lifelong partner! But when it came to choosing my husband, I had never experienced such confidence and certainty in my entire life. It was obvious that he was my person. However, I don't think I could have had this assurance without going through my big breakup first and learning from my love lessons. With my ex, I thought it was normal to be unsure, to have my inner voice nagging at me, to rationalize my reasoning to remain in the relationship; but with my husband, all I experienced was clarity and an alignment of our values, life goals, and personalities. I was living authentically in this relationship, and it felt right in my gut.

The painstaking truth is that just because you're in love with someone or have incredible sex, or are both stellar individuals independently, doesn't mean that you're the best long-term partners and should make it work. Things get even more complex when there are external factors, such as sharing kids or co-owning a property or business, being close with their family, or having financial security together. I hate the inspirational quotes on Pinterest that say "Love conquers all," or "All you need is love." Um, no. You need ingredients like effective communication, aligned core values, shared life goals, compatible personalities, commitment, the practice of gratitude, empathy, and effort. Lovin' feelings and physical attraction will only get you so far. Don't feel that you *must* make it work just because you *could* make it work. Be wary of slipping into the status "quople" dynamic in future relationships. This book is all about letting go, dating smarter, and creating the love life you deserve, so use the list below of status "quople" warning signs to inform your dating decisions moving forward.

STATUS "QUOPLE" RED FLAGS

- ♥ You are living parallel lives.
- ♥ You feel more like roommates than lovers.
- ♥ You have sex but the emotional intimacy is long gone.
- ♥ You often feel as though your needs are unmet.

♥ You're not working toward joint goals.

♥ You try to bring up conversations about your future together but your partner dodges them.

♥ Your heart and head want different things.

♥ You find yourself fantasizing or wishing that your partner will change.

♥ You intentionally seek out attention from other people or consider having an affair.

Checking off one of these boxes alone doesn't mean you're a status "quople," but it does represent a crack in the foundation of your relationship that needs to be addressed ASAP. Though it's too late for a relationship that just ended, I'd hate for you to get stuck in this pattern with someone new. We enter into relationships with our own expectations and needs, yet no one has the magical ability to mind-read, so it's your responsibility to ask for what you want. If your partner can't meet these needs, chooses to ignore them, or belittles you for being needy, then this is valuable information that should inform your conscious decision to remain in the relationship or leave. Clear communication in a couples dynamic should be focused on your *own* emotions or behaviors. For instance, if you're feeling a lack of chemistry and connection, and the flirtation has fizzled, an appropriate comment to your partner might be, "I noticed that I've been feeling disconnected lately. Quality time makes me feel loved and close to you. Can we carve out some time on our calendars for a weekly date night?" At the end of the day, you have to ask for what you need from your partner. There's a quote from an unknown author that I'd like you to keep in mind when it comes to status "quople" relationships: "Alone doesn't always mean lonely. Relationship doesn't always mean happy. Being alone will never cause as much loneliness as being in the wrong relationship."

Cultivating Self-Love and Creating New Purpose

Take a moment to reflect on what you've learned since cracking the cover of this book. Holy guacamole, you've already taken enormous steps forward. Cue 2001 and play some Destiny's Child because you are a survivor. Beyoncé would be so proud of you! You've learned to:

- ♥ Identify your emotions and sit with them, and how to move through the stages of grief.

- ♥ Prioritize yourself, invest in self-care, and maintain healthy habits for sleep, eating, and exercise.

- ♥ Stop the damaging hanging-on hookup behavior, cut off cold turkey, and set firm breakup boundaries.

- ♥ Employ a no-contact rule to give your brain and body time and space to cool off and fall out of love.

- ♥ Utilize mindfulness skills, such as deep breathing with your breakup mantra, and set rumination limits with your dwell spell.

- ♥ Be more mindful of your automatic negative thoughts, which impact your mood, behaviors, actions, and, ultimately, reality.

- ♥ Determine your attachment style and how it ties into your adult romantic relationships.

- ♥ Gain insight into the reasons behind your breakup, such as conflicting love languages and core values, and you're aware of falling into the trap of a status "quople."

- ♥ Reflect on your love lessons and explore old emotional injuries that no longer serve you on your love journey.

- ♥ Take steps to rewrite a more positive narrative for love.

On a scale from 1 to 10, with 1 = heart shattered and 10 = fully healed, where do you currently fall? If you're not where you'd like to be, don't forget that we all move through this at a different pace, and remember you can revisit the tough love quotes from chapter 4 when you need that extra motivation. Continue to be kind and compassionate with yourself, as you're well on your way to mending that big, loving heart of yours.

CHAPTER 10

Self-Love Is the Best Love

The quality of your romantic relationship is directly related to your own sense of self. Your partner is a mirror who reflects back the version of you that's most prevalent in the relationship. When you were with your ex, did you recognize yourself? Do you like who you were? Were you proud or ashamed of yourself?

Having a strong sense of self, which may have been lost or muddied in your last relationship, is essential to creating a love that lasts for the long run. In fact, it helps us in every area: with friends, family, and colleagues as well. When you don't like yourself or know who you are, you tend to fall into codependent, superficial relationships. You probably won't like who you see when you look in the mirror of that relationship. It's also one thing to know yourself, and another thing to love yourself. We are a constant work in progress, but self-love happens when you let go of your perceived flaws and how others define you and you begin to embrace your authentic self as enough. You can love yourself even if you aren't "whole" or still have work to do. Self-love means embracing imperfections, weaknesses, and wounds. You also don't need to be perfect spiritually, mentally, and emotionally in order to find love. It can be very healing to add a romantic partner to the mix, who can soothe you and build you up. It's a balance, however, of not being completely reliant on your partner to heal these wounds, and being accountable to your own self-improvement work. Because we inherently depend on others for belonging, we can't build self-love in a vacuum by ourselves.

In *The Gifts of Imperfection*, Brené Brown says, "Practicing self-love means learning how to trust ourselves, to treat ourselves with respect, and to be kind and affectionate toward ourselves." To cultivate a healthy, fulfilling relationship where both partners feel at their best begins when you put effort into loving yourself. Developing and maintaining this foundation of self-love is essential whether your're single or in a relationship. The biggest barriers to self-love are not feeling good enough, wasting your time comparing yourself to others, and living by other people's standards instead of the ones you choose and accept for yourself. Follow the tips below to begin practicing self-love, it's as simple as that!

HOW TO PRACTICE SELF-LOVE

- ♥ Speak kindly, sweetly, and compassionately to yourself; be your biggest fan and lay off the self-deprecating humor.

- ♥ Utilize daily affirmations to affirm your worthiness and appreciate the ways in which you are special and unique.

- ♥ Stop trying so hard to be like everybody else; define what you think is admirable, beautiful, cool, sexy, and fun (be aware of the messages you've internalized as a child, whether from your parents, your friends, or the TV shows you watched; and remember as an adult you can redefine yourself, whenever and however you want).

- ♥ Surround yourself with a support system who encourages, motivates, and cheers you on to be the best version of yourself.

- ♥ Take time to recharge your battery.

- ♥ Eat foods that energize and heal you.

- ♥ Move your body in ways that give you strength, flexibility, and confidence.

- ♥ Spend and save your money in line with your values.

- ♥ Make choices that are aligned with who you want to be.

The world will see you
the way you see you,
and treat you the way
you treat yourself.

BEYONCÉ

♥ Praise yourself for your strengths and accept your imperfections.

♥ Say no and set boundaries with people or things that try to bring you down or conflict with how you want to live your life.

♥ Do activities that fill you with joy. When is the last time you actually did the thing that you think of when someone asks you, "What makes you feel alive?"

♥ Step away from people-pleasing and focus on your own wants and needs.

♥ Practice gratitude.

♥ Prioritize your goals, challenge yourself even in the face of failure, and do things that inspire you.

♥ Make decisions that honor your truth, embrace your intuition, trust your gut, and take the role of expert in your own life.

♥ Believe that happiness is not having the best of everything you want, it's making the best of everything you have.

♥ Forgive yourself for the mistakes you make and choose to let go of bad feelings.

♥ Realize that for all of the time you waste thinking negative thoughts, you could give this same attention to positive ones.

♥ As much as possible, try to live life in the present instead of dwelling on the past or worrying about the future.

♥ Commit to creating the life you envision.

♥ Realize self-love is not about perfection or looking and acting a certain way, but a reflection of how you embrace and honor your own heart, soul, and personality, allowing yourself to be seen.

This is your time to focus on yourself and not have to worry about meeting the needs of someone else. Maybe you secretly hated your ex's friends or dreaded the times they got to pick the weekend activities. The perks of a breakup are that you're the boss now. Self-love looks good on you.

EXERCISE: I AM WORTHY

Grab your Bounce Back Journal and answer the following questions:

- ♥ If you believed you're worthy of love, how would you treat yourself differently? What parts and traits would you appreciate more?

- ♥ If you believed you're worthy of love, how would you speak to yourself differently? What words would you stop using (examples *should, always, never*) and what names would you stop calling yourself?

- ♥ If you believed you're worthy of love, what self-care would you engage in regularly?

- ♥ If you believed you're worthy of love, how would your behavior and interactions with romantic interests change?

- ♥ If you believed you're worthy of love, what personality qualities and values would a partner have to possess in order for you to date them?

- ♥ If you believed you're worthy of love, how would your partner treat you?

- ♥ If you believed you're worthy of love, what boundaries would you set so that you don't accept anything less than you deserve?

The bad news is that your heart has been broken, but the good news is that you can heal it for a new opportunity to find love. Before looking outwards in your search for a more ideal match, you need to turn your attention inwards to truly grasp this fresh start. What you'll find when you listen to your body and mind is an underlying inner voice. Practicing self-love means embracing your intuition, which is your inner knowing. You may have heard it when something felt off during your relationship, when you were trying to figure out if your ex was The One, the voice that ultimately told you to initiate the breakup or the one that's telling you right now that it would've never worked.

You're the best expert on yourself. Only you know when your needs aren't being met, or something feels off. Empower that intuition rather than stuff it down. During your relationship with your ex, did your inner voice ever tell you that you weren't happy, that your ex was not the best fit for you, or that you deserved more? What are the thoughts and feelings that you pushed down as you trudged forward in your relationship, pretending it would all work itself out? They're likely tied to your emotional injuries from childhood, rooted in fear, shame, hurt, and vulnerability. Think of your inner voice as your more enlightened, protective adult who is trying to help you break free from negative patterns and limiting beliefs. It's a wise guide that can help you challenge your dysfunctional and destructive deep-seated assumptions.

Your inner voice represents intuition on a gut level—it's your self-protection. You typically hear an underlying message or feel a sense of what's right, but sometimes you try to intellectualize your choices that go against this gut feeling. We live in our brain instead of our body. Often, in the wrong relationship you try to convince yourself *not* to listen to that inner voice because it's not the outcome you want. "What do you mean break up with him? He's hot, and the sex is good, he's going to start treating me better, I just need to stick it out . . ." But here's the thing, you've been created for survival and your gut feeling exists to keep you safe from physical and emotional harm. Trust your intuition, even if it doesn't make sense or isn't the outcome you're hoping for. Respect yourself enough to know that deep down you know what's best, so allow that to lead rather than your head trash.

Trusting in your inner voice means you acknowledge that you invested in a relationship that was not ideal or healthy, that you settled for comfort and compromise instead of seeking out what you really desired or deserved, and that you ultimately did not value and honor your worth. These can be hard pills to swallow, but learning to listen to this voice will help you meet your needs and set appropriate boundaries, and you'll be better able to catch red flags in future relationships. Sometimes your inner voice takes the form of not liking yourself, like when you're feeling needy, insecure, crazy, jealous, or sad; crying all of the time; not feeling good enough; or fighting with your partner more often than you get along. These red flags should signal to you that you're behaving in a way that validates your emotional injuries and false assumptions. A relationship that elicits these emotions may feel familiar, but it's not bringing out the best in you. It's your job to notice these dynamics and emotions, and take action.

I now want you to compile and combine all that you've learned and reflected upon, especially from the love lessons learned and the emotional injuries exercises explored in chapter 7 to forge a letter of self-forgiveness. You can't love yourself when you can't forgive yourself. Go back and revisit the questions from those exercises for inspiration.

EXERCISE: WRITE A SELF-FORGIVENESS LETTER

- ♥ Write a letter to yourself in which you recognize and acknowledge the mistakes you made in your relationship, including the poor ways in which you treated your partner and yourself. Write, "I forgive myself."

- ♥ Reflect on the emotional injuries you have tried to heal since childhood, and the erroneous beliefs you internalized about love. Remember that at the time these helped you to make sense of the world and ways in which you were wounded. Acknowledge that these destructive assumptions no longer serve you. Write, "I forgive myself for behaving in ways and repeating patterns that validated my destructive assumptions." At this point you may also be able to ask yourself if you can forgive those who wounded you too, releasing blame and resentment from your heart.

- ♥ Next, identify and write down the new ways in which you'll treat yourself with love, value, and respect. Write, "In moving forward with my life, I'm committed to making these changes and creating a new narrative for love."

You can return to this letter and reread it as often as you'd like, especially if you relapse in your breakup grief, or as you begin to date new people. Allow this self-forgiveness letter to bring you closure and serve as a new framework for healthy, secure, adult love. Your ability to heal and find closure was in you all along.

CHAPTER 11

———♥———→

Getting Back Out There

It's time to reenter the market and girl, let me tell you, you have a lot to offer! There's no correct answer about how long after a breakup you should wait until you begin dating again. This entire process is about listening to your gut and intuition and trusting that you know yourself best. You may need to challenge and push yourself, and the worst case is you go on a date and it reinforces that you're not ready yet. If your heart isn't in it, take some more time to heal and focus on self-care and your new goals. Some people like to dip a toe in and slowly acclimate to the temperature, whereas others cannonball in with a splash. Regardless if you're a slow mover or you take the dating scene by storm, you're going to get out of your dating and love life what you put into it.

When I say it's time to start dating again, what is your reaction? Take a few moments to tune into your mind and body. When you think about dating again, where do you feel it in your body? Does your heart flutter or race? Do you get a sinking feeling in your gut? Grab your Bounce Back Journal and reflect on the following questions:

EXERCISE: MY AUTOMATIC REACTIONS TO DATING

- ♥ My automatic thoughts about dating are . . .
- ♥ My automatic feelings about dating are . . .
- ♥ My physical reaction to the idea of dating is . . .

126

Keep in mind that just because you begin dating again it doesn't mean you need to become exclusive or committed with someone and enter into another relationship right away. First you need to become an expert on yourself, knowing and understanding your personality traits, labeling and honoring your deal breakers, and having a crystal clear vision of what's most important to you. All of this takes time to figure out, so if you're not ready to dive in full steam ahead with dating, there's still plenty of proactive work you can be doing in your love life. This will prepare you to find a complimentary partner that aligns well with your needs and desires. That way, once you get back in the game, you can do so intentionally so that you're only entering into exclusive, committed relationships with people that demonstrate that they have those traits and core values of your ideal match.

Some nervousness around the idea of opening up to someone again is totally normal and something you can work through. It's possible to overcome dating fears. You're embarking on an important next chapter in your life, and approaching it with an open and optimistic attitude is going to make an enormous difference. If you're filled with dread or cynicism, you'll likely attract other Debbie Downers with pessimistic, negative attitudes. Do they sound fun to date? No! We attract people with a similar energy. I don't want to get too spiritual on you, since I tend to be a woman of science, but there's something to be said for a belief in an interconnection of energy. In *You Are a Badass,* Jen Sincero writes, "All energy vibrates at a certain frequency. Which means you're vibrating at a certain frequency, and everything you desire and don't desire, is also vibrating at a certain frequency. Vibration attracts like vibration . . . We're all attracting energy to ourselves all the time whether we realize it or not. And when we're vibrating at a low frequency (feeling pessimistic, needy, victimized, jealous, shameful, worried, convinced we are ugly) yet expect high frequency, awesome things and experiences to come into our lives, we are often disappointed . . . The Universe will match whatever vibration you put out. And you can't fool The Universe."

A hugely important mind-set shift you can make is to move from one of fear and scarcity (I will get my heart broken again, there are no good men out there, I suck at dating) to a mind-set of hope and abundance (there are so many men out there who will love me, someone will love all that I am, I believe I am worthy of reciprocal love). As you prepare to date again, make a conscious effort to exude confidence and positivity, and set your intentions for meeting an incredible, wholehearted partner who can show you the love that you deserve. I know it can be scary to even admit you want to find love again, because then you'll feel all vulnerable, like you'll jinx it, or feel shame when you don't find it right away. But setting your intentions and owning what you want without diminishing your goals is a very important step to opening yourself up to attract and receive it.

When you believe your ideal match is out there, they will be. When you imagine what it feels like to receive the love you want, and then go about your day operating from this place as though you're already receiving that magnificent love, you'll be operating from a higher energy and more likely to attract it. Catch and challenge your negative thoughts so that you can replace the fear with belief and hope. Believe that everything you want already exists and is available to you. Feel confident that you have the power to pick who you want to be with rather than settling or choosing people who will validate your old narrative. Know that you're a catch, and believe there's an equally amazing partner out there who'll cherish you. Pick up your pen, it's time for another exercise.

EXERCISE: MY FIVE BIGGEST DATING FEARS

In your Bounce Back Journal, I want you to identify your top five biggest dating fears. Here are some examples to get you started:

- ♥ I'll get my heart broken again.
- ♥ I won't find anyone who I like more than my ex.
- ♥ I will be alone forever.
- ♥ No one will be attracted to me.
- ♥ I feel awkward meeting someone that I don't know.

1. _____

2. _____

3. _____

4. _____

5. _____

First, don't judge yourself for having these fears. Next, I want you to challenge each negative thought with a positive reframe. This can be tricky, since these fears are deep-rooted. If you're stumped, pretend your best friend is going through this breakup and she just told you all of the same fears. How would you respond to her? Here are some examples to get you started:

- ♥ I'll get my heart broken again: Reframe = This fear is not helping me receive the love I truly want. I have to be vulnerable to find love.

- ♥ I won't find anyone who I like more than my ex: Reframe = There's an abundance of men out there, I just need to be active and open in my dating life to meet them. I choose to welcome new, interesting, generous, caring people into my life.

- ♥ I will be alone forever: Reframe = I know I will find a connection, I just haven't met him yet. I will remain open to receiving love and be proactive in searching for it.

- ♥ No one will be attracted to me: Reframe = I accept that not everyone will be attracted to me, the same way I'm not attracted to every guy I meet, and that doesn't make me unworthy or unattractive. I am beautiful and deserve to find someone who desires me. I will only focus my attention on suitors who find me attractive instead of chasing men who seem disinterested.

- ♥ I feel awkward meeting someone that I don't know: Reframe = It's normal to be nervous, but I know I can offer so much to a partner. I want and deserve love, so I will honor myself and am committed to opening my heart and being vulnerable with potential partners.

Now try creating your own responses to counter the fears you listed:

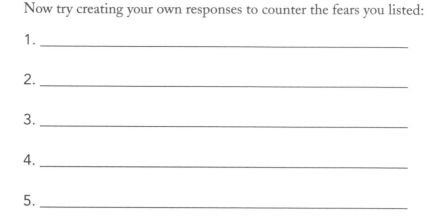

1. _____

2. _____

3. _____

4. _____

5. _____

Good job! Anytime you notice a fear holding you back or bringing you down, write it down and challenge it with a more positive, realistic statement. You can reread these statements as often as necessary to start believing them. This powerful cognitive behavioral technique helps you gain more control over your automatic negative thoughts, which are free-flowing and we mistakenly treat as fact. Sometimes we are our own worst enemies, and treating negative thoughts as facts doesn't serve us, especially when we're trying to rebuild our lives, increase our self-esteem, and open ourselves up to attracting and receiving even greater love. If your thoughts aren't aligned with your desires, you're unwittingly keeping yourself stuck. For instance, "I want love, but I'm unlovable." Can you see how that's damaging, sends the wrong energy out into the universe, and doesn't set you up for success? The law of attraction says that if you focus on positive or negative thoughts, you'll bring either positive or negative experiences into your life. You're unconsciously sending wrong desires into the universe with your stinkin' thinkin', and this energy will only bring people into your life who also don't value your worth. You must align your thoughts and desires. A positive reframe would be, "I want love and I deserve a partner who loves me unconditionally."

EXERCISE: ARE YOU READY TO DATE?

Let's assess your readiness and willingness to make changes and put yourself back out there. Rate the following on a scale from 1 to 10 (10 = extremely):

♥ How important is dating to you right now?

♥ How motivated are you to date again?

♥ What's your confidence in dating?

If you rated dating importance as less than a 5, it's clearly not a priority in your life right now, or you might still feel too damaged from your last relationship. Wherever you are in your journey is okay, some people hit a wall at this point and may need a little extra nudging or cheerleading. You want to be at a point where you've created a rewarding life for yourself with supportive friends, hobbies, and interests, but don't forget that we also get a sense of worthiness and belonging through a romantic relationship. You don't have to be one hundred percent healed or whole to find love. The next step in your journey is to make dating a priority. You bought this book not just to survive but to thrive, and there's bigger and better things waiting for you! I know deep down you believe in finding love again. If dating importance is high, but your motivation is low, ask yourself what might get you one point higher on the motivation scale. This means you'll have to identify any barriers to motivation, and then take action to work on one concrete thing that's in the way. Your low motivation could be tied to your confidence. We'll tackle confidence and how to develop a healthy dating mind-set in the upcoming chapters.

If you worry that it's too soon to get out on the market again, you may be exercising too much caution. In *Why Him, Why Her*, Dr. Helen Fisher discusses the importance of timing in finding love. We're more susceptible to finding romantic love during big life transitions, such as after a breakup or divorce, a move, starting a new job, or going to college. Fisher highlights that transitions produce stress and strong emotions, which can escalate the feelings of passion. She writes, "As you struggle through one of life's upheavals, the circuits in your brain for general arousal, energy, focus and motivation can push you closer to the threshold for falling in love." The expression "The best way to get over someone is to get under someone else" must come from somewhere, right? Your body is physically primed to fall in love. And now is the time to create space in your life for a new romance with its own traditions, rituals, inside jokes, and neurochemical responses that leave you feeling giddy.

If I am the longest
relationship of my life,
isn't it time to nurture
intimacy and love with
the person I lie in bed
with each night?

RUPI KAUR

CHAPTER 12

Here I Am

One of the hardest things about a breakup can be how it disrupts your vision of the future. It feels disappointing and frustrating when you haven't met your life timelines, such as getting engaged or married by a certain age, or when a divorce means having to start over again. Take a deep breath and tell yourself, "Let go." These timelines are artificial—you created them because you told yourself you *should* be at a certain point by a certain time. But these *shoulds* aren't facts. The reality is you can't control everything. Rather than stressing about not being where you envisioned and beating yourself up, give yourself permission to let go of this pressure.

Imagine that you're standing in front of a giant chalkboard with all of the life milestones you haven't yet met. Begin erasing each expectation that is causing you stress. Goodbye "married by thirty," adios "my friends are engaged so I should be too," so long "I'm afraid to be alone so I'll take what I can get!" Now, picture yourself standing in front of a clean, blank board. Envision yourself covering the entire board with all of your amazing accomplishments and qualities. Maybe you're proud of your sense of humor, your tenacious work ethic, your ability to make people laugh, your hard-earned work promotion, the time you traveled independently in a foreign country, your ability to be there for your friends, or your resiliency for surviving a traumatic loss. Let yourself revel in all that you are. *Without the pressure of those artificial timelines, how can you live your life embodying the traits and characteristics that you love about yourself?*

If you found it challenging to fill up the chalkboard with your endearing qualities, either you don't value yourself enough or you're too modest! Confidence is one of the most attractive qualities in dating because it suggests that you're secure in who you are—your body, your interests, your beliefs, your goals. But don't confuse confidence with being cocky.

EXERCISE: WHY I'M F*$#ING FABULOUS

Take a time out from reading this book and text or call a few of your closest friends. Remember, we can't cultivate self-love in a vacuum. Tell them you're redefining the way you view yourself. Ask from their perspective what they admire most about you, and what they consider to be your best strengths and qualities. After their feedback, I want you to say, "I gracefully accept your compliments," rather than refuting anything. Write down whatever descriptions or adjectives they share with you in your Bounce Back Journal. Were you surprised by any of their responses? Is it difficult to see yourself in this light? Accept, embrace, and embody these new flattering qualities. Underneath your friends' descriptions, create a new section in your journal and answer the following questions:

♥ What are my strongest or best attributes? List at least ten. Consider the following adjectives for inspiration:

Friendly	Courageous	Compassionate
Silly	Assertive	Caring
Brilliant	Charismatic	Reliable
Hilarious	Positive	Resilient
Thoughtful	Kind	Patient
Gracious	Creative	Loyal
Benevolent	Responsible	Cultured
Charitable	Dependable	Intelligent
Loving	Honest	Driven
Affectionate	Energetic	Passionate
Confident	Sexy	Soulful
Spiritual	Bubbly	Empathetic
Educated	Steadfast	Persistent

- ♥ What am I most passionate about?
- ♥ What do I love the most about my mind?
- ♥ What do I love the most about my body?
- ♥ What life accomplishments am I the most proud of?
- ♥ What do I offer a romantic partner? (Make sure to include things you are, things you do, and things you have.)

As you grow more confident and develop a stronger sense of self, revisit your journal entry and add in new adjectives or qualities that you adore about yourself.

Because one of the most attractive qualities in a romantic partner is confidence, potential partners are looking for that same self-confidence in you. To be confident is to have faith in yourself, to respect, appreciate, admire, and honor yourself. When you own your worth, you behave with integrity and feel proud of your words and actions. When you don't like how you treat others or treat yourself, you start to think that you deserve less. If you criticize and judge yourself harshly, you're sending out energy that repels quality partners who would respect and value you. You begin to settle or punish yourself and put up with less than you deserve because you don't think you are worth more. Without confidence, you let others treat you poorly, those who don't cherish you, who cheat, who abuse, who don't make you a priority, and who don't meet your needs. You are even cruel to yourself, whether by engaging in negative self-talk, abusing your body with drugs or alcohol, binge eating or depriving yourself of nutrients, exercising too much or too little, or surrounding yourself with the wrong people.

In short, when you lack self-confidence, you don't think you deserve the best. So, I'm asking you right now, on a scale from 1 to 10 (10 = totally obsessed), how confident are you in yourself? Do you despise, like, or love yourself? Does it depend on the day, your weight, your hair, or what kind of attention you're getting from men? There are many ways and sources from which to cultivate confidence, but typically the first one that comes to mind is physical attractiveness. We spend so much time hating our bodies, enviously comparing ourselves to supermodels or fashionistas pinning lust-worthy photos featuring their imperfectly perfect messy buns, thigh gaps,

Love yourself first and everything else falls into line. You really have to love yourself to get anything done in this world.

LUCILLE BALL

and trendy #OOTD (it took me a while to figure out that meant "outfit of the day"). These unrealistic representations present themselves as the norm when they're actually an unattainable ideal; but exposure to them takes us farther and farther away from self-acceptance as we focus on fitting into societal standards of beauty, rather than belonging.

Well, here's a news flash for you: creating lasting love isn't about how hot you are. In fact, when researchers explored how physical attractiveness impacts relationships, the results weren't positive. In a series of studies, Christine Ma-Kellams and her colleagues found that those people who were rated as more attractive in high school yearbooks were married for a shorter time and more likely to divorce. The same findings were true for top male and female celebrities. The researchers concluded that physical attractiveness predicts shorter relationships, and that these individuals put in less effort to maintain their partnerships because they believed they had more alternative options in their dating pool. Even though being attractive attracted mates in the first place, from a relationship-maintenance perspective, physical attractiveness was actually a cost to the relationship itself.

So rather than trying to fix yourself by focusing on all of the external "imperfections," work on loving and accepting yourself as is. Imagine how freeing it would be to not feel like you have to change yourself, to not hate yourself, and to be enough right now—all of that pressure just disappears. When it comes to dating, there's so much more to you than your looks, such as kindness, loyalty, understanding, conscientiousness, and emotional stability, and loving with an open heart. The more you focus on what you love about yourself, the more self-love you will actually have. The more you try to be someone you're not, the farther you get from feeling good enough. Things like makeup, how you do your hair, or the clothes you choose to adorn your body shouldn't be looked at as ways to "fix" yourself, but rather as a representation of the love you have for yourself.

If you have low self-esteem, hate your body, don't value or respect yourself, and feel unlovable then the partners you attract probably won't value and respect you either. On the flip side, if you're confident, self-assured, embrace your inner and outer beauty and feel worthy of love, then a partner will cherish and value all that you bring to the table. The thing is, *you* control who you show up as when you arrive at the table by changing your beliefs about yourself and love. It's not thinking "if I do ABC, *then* I'll be lovable." Instead, it's about identifying what you don't love about yourself, and rather than feeling you have to frantically change these qualities, choosing to love yourself anyway. Eleanor Roosevelt again for the win: "No one can make you feel inferior without your consent." When you can accept and love yourself, "flaws" and all, someone else can too.

As you start dating again, use all of your newfound confidence and willingness to be vulnerable to pursue only dates who are worth your time. I often hear clients talk about how the person they're seeing is a "good guy" because he doesn't cheat, he plans dates, and he might even give you a compliment. In my book, that alone doesn't qualify someone as a good guy. Someone who's faithful, puts effort into taking you out, and who makes you feel attractive should be the underlying requirements for dating someone—this makes him a "basic guy" and everyone else out there is just subpar if they don't meet these relationship standards. When you own your worth, you'll settle for nothing less. Do you believe there are actually good, quality partners out there who don't lie, cheat, control, degrade, or devalue you? You have to believe this, even if you haven't dated one before, otherwise you'll continue to attract dating duds.

Think back to the attachment styles I outlined. The secure partner is the perfect example of how you deserve to be treated. They'll be consistent in pursuing you and giving you attention, welcoming intimacy and embracing closeness, letting you know what page they're on, and openly communicating about feelings. What makes someone an exceptional or "good guy" are the ways they speak your love language, how they prioritize you when obligations pull them in different directions, and all of their unique qualities that compliment your own traits and make them the ideal match for you. What do you deserve when it comes to a romantic partner? When you date from a place of confidence and worth, and shift away from a place of shame and scarcity, you'll have total control over your love life.

EXERCISE: I DESERVE SOMEONE WHO . . .

How do you want to feel in your next relationship? When you love and respect yourself, what do you expect out of a partner? Take out your Bounce Back Journal and create a list of what you deserve. Here are some ideas to get you started:

- ♥ I deserve someone who prioritizes my happiness.
- ♥ I deserve someone who really listens when I talk about my day.

- ♥ I deserve someone who includes me in their social plans.

- ♥ I deserve someone who makes decisions as a team.

- ♥ I deserve someone who takes the time to develop emotional intimacy instead of hopping into bed.

- ♥ I deserve someone who also shows up vulnerably in the relationship.

- ♥ I deserve someone who _____.

Add as many as you can think of.

Use these statements, which honor your needs and desires, to set intentions as you begin to date again. Although, you can certainly find a relationship if you feel insecure, worthless, or unworthy, it won't be healthy and won't make you happy in the long run. If you've been adhering to your self-care and creating purpose by investing in your emotional, physical, social, spiritual, and environmental goals, then you should be on your way to feeling good and glowing with confidence.

A QUICK NOTE ON COMPARING YOUR NEW SUITORS TO YOUR EX

It's easy to remember all of the wonderful things about your ex and forget the heartache they caused you when you're comparing them to the new people you're dating. Stop idolizing your ex; they weren't perfect. It's time to take them off the pedestal and dethrone them. When you begin dating, you'll likely start by comparing every new person you meet to your ex. Comparison is normal, but it's unrealistic to think that you'll find or create a Frankenboyfriend who has all of the desirable qualities your ex was lacking pieced together with the parts that you cherished about them the most. When you're looking backwards you'll never really be able to see and accept someone new. So, do yourself a huge favor and take off your rose-colored glasses that falsely lead you to believe your ex had no flaws. Of course there were great things about them; otherwise you wouldn't have dated them. But note the word dated—past tense because it didn't work out.

CHAPTER 13

Realistic Dating Mind-sets

You've accepted that your breakup wasn't a failure, but rather an opportunity and even a wake-up call for how you want to be treated in a future relationship. You're motivated to get back out there and find your ideal match. Yet, the thought of being hurt again makes you want to build a bulletproof wall around your heart to prevent it from being shattered into a million pieces. How have you been running away from love? Do you sit at home instead of attending social events to avoid interacting with new people? How about swiping mindlessly on dating apps for an ego boost, with no real intention to meet up? Do you make excuses about why no one is good enough for you and complain there are no quality partners out there? Are you guilty of leading with overtly sexualized behavior, such as sending sexual messages and images, or sleeping together too soon? What about agreeing to Netflix-and-chill nights with the person you know has no potential? If these sound familiar, you're lacking vulnerability.

EMBRACING VULNERABILITY

Have you ever heard the word *intimacy* rephrased into *into-me-see*? The first time I saw this, I thought of it in terms of allowing someone else to see deeply into you. What I realized in writing this is that intimacy doesn't start with a connection to your partner. It begins with a connection to yourself. Being intimate with yourself means looking inwards to see your old wounds and emotional injuries, insecurities, and shame. Amongst these dark feelings lies the most powerful experience when it comes to dating, and that's *vulnerability*.

Being truly intimate with yourself means embracing and honoring your vulnerabilities as strengths, rather than burying them, overcompensating, or putting up defenses. When you've suffered from one relationship falling apart (or several), you worry about exposing yourself to the same devastation again. We build defenses, like armor, around our emotional injuries that prevent us from showing up in all of our vulnerable glory. Defenses such as self-deflecting or self-deprecating humor, anger, and being a know-it-all, people-pleaser, or perfectionist are meant to protect us from the awful feelings of our wounds.

We project our own flaws and insecurities onto the people we date. For example, perfectionists are intolerant of their own imperfections, which means they're not living authentically or vulnerably. In their dating lives, they'll never find a "perfect" partner or fairy-tale love life because they're intolerant of everyone else's imperfections too. They project all of their own disappointments, dissatisfaction, and disgust onto the people they attract into their lives. Know-it-alls are the type of people who claim to have tried and done everything in their love lives. They tend to be impatient and state that nothing works, clinging to an idea of what a relationship *should* be. Though they may come across as confident and secure on the surface, they operate from a place of fear and self-doubt, attracting partners who are also insecure.

These defensive behaviors take attention away from us, so that we can hide our shame. Instead we place the focus on other people's flaws–she's too chubby, he's too short, they don't meet all of my unspoken expectations. Hiding behind our defenses only breeds more shame and keeps us stuck in our dysfunctional narratives, instead of truly connecting with others. But when you allow yourself to be vulnerable in your dating life, which means not hiding or trying to be someone you're not, something beautiful and magnetic happens. You show up as the most authentic version of yourself. And when you date from an authentic place, this is when you attract someone with the best version of yourself, creating real, deep connection and intimacy.

Having your wounds kissed
by someone who doesn't
see them as disasters in
your soul, but cracks to put
their love into, is the most
calming thing in this world.

EMERY ALLEN

When you allow someone to see you as you are (for instance, when you show up to a date at your current weight instead of your goal weight, or you show up not having yet earned the promotion you want, which you think defines your success), instead of as who you want to be or force yourself to be, you're allowing that person to connect with you in all of your vulnerability and authenticity. Vulnerability is the connection, intimacy, and belonging that you've always desired in a relationship, with no strings attached. I say no strings attached because when you show up as enough, you don't have to try to be anything other than yourself.

For one person, vulnerability means sharing underlying shame stories and fears, whereas for another being vulnerable means no longer engaging in self-sabotaging behaviors and negative patterns. Being vulnerable does not mean dumping all of your past hurts and traumas onto the table on a first date, but instead understanding how you've been hurt and keeping your heart open to love despite the potential to be hurt again. Being vulnerable means letting someone in and allowing them to help you, even if you're self-sufficient and can do it on your own. Being vulnerable means believing and having faith that you're worthy of fulfilling faithful love, even if you haven't received it in the past. Being vulnerable means not settling for less than you deserve, even when you're tempted to put up with someone who isn't meeting your needs because you desperately want to be loved.

Typically our defenses develop early in life due to painful experiences with family and friends, and we continue to use them in hurtful romantic relationship experiences. Below is a five-step exercise that will help you lower your defenses, embrace vulnerability, and claim your worth so that you can live more authentically and be more intimate with yourself and a partner.

EXERCISE: TAKING OFF YOUR ARMOR TO EMBRACE YOUR AUTHENTIC SELF

1. **Identify your underlying emotional injury from early in life (think of painful experiences with caregivers or friends).** Example: Meredith's mom always compared her to her sister, whether it was her height and weight, the foods she ate, or her positions on sports teams. Meredith never felt she could win her mom's approval, and remembers feeling sad that her mother infrequently said "I love you."

2. **Label your internalized beliefs and false assumptions about yourself and love.** Example: Meredith identified that she seeks a lot of external validation because she never feels good enough, and deep down worries no one will ever really love her. Since dating apps became more popular, it has only diminished Meredith's confidence and self-worth, since she assumed there were prettier women out there with superior profiles. This automatically made her feel like she was in second place, similar to her feelings of being compared to her sister when she was a child.

3. **Identify your defense mechanism(s), which are the ways you protect yourself or have learned to deal with the false assumptions you discussed above.** Example: Meredith's defense mechanism was to become a *people-pleaser* in hopes of gaining approval. At her job she would overwork herself because she wanted to be recognized and praised by her boss. In her romantic relationships, she would people-please by putting her own needs on the back burner and invest more effort and energy in men that never seemed to reciprocate her affection. The more they pulled away, the more effort she invested, thinking they'd come around and realize how amazing she was and never want to let her go. She felt like she was doing everything possible to be liked, whether that meant clearing her schedule to be available when they asked her on a date, or sleeping with guys early on because she thought that's what they wanted and assumed they'd know that if she was sleeping with them that it meant she liked them and wanted to be in a relationship. She also went out of her way to do sweet gestures, like bake brownies and pick out small gifts for the men in her life, yet they rarely did anything special for her. Although she desperately wanted to be someone's girlfriend and to get married, men would leave her after a few weeks or months of dating for what Meredith assumed was someone better. Despite her efforts to win men's affection, they didn't seem to choose her.

4. **Examine how your defense mechanism prevents real vulnerability.**
Example: For Meredith, people-pleasing prevented her from living authentically and asking for what she truly desired—a committed, exclusive relationship. Because she was so focused on making the men she was dating happy, she wasn't making herself happy. She worried that if she asked questions like "Where is this relationship going?" she would be viewed as needy and would push men away. Her attempts to prove herself as enough backfired and she never got what she hoped for. The people-pleasing prevented Meredith from valuing herself, making her expectations clear, and setting the standards for how she wanted to be treated. She didn't show her real needs or feelings, and instead tried to be who she thought other people wanted.

5. **Take off your armor and reject your defenses by identifying ways to be more vulnerable in order to bring more intimacy into your life.** Example: To Meredith, being vulnerable meant only behaving in ways that aligned with her goals of entering into an exclusive relationship. Instead of people-pleasing and seeking approval from anyone that would give her attention, she committed to only giving as much to a romantic interest as he was giving to her. If he wasn't putting in enough effort, she'd move on to someone that was willing to make her a priority. This meant only going out with men who made plans in advance to see her, only texting or talking on the phone with men who carried on meaningful conversations where they asked questions and seemed genuinely interested in getting to know her, and refusing to sext or send nudes or sleep with someone unless they agreed to be monogamous. Meredith also committed to making plans with friends at least twice per week and refused to blow off these plans to accommodate a date. By setting these boundaries, Meredith was able to meet Griffin, who asked her to be his girlfriend after five dates. They have been dating eight months now and have exchanged "I love you's." Meredith is happier than ever before because she honored her desire for a relationship. This allowed her to date more authentically and attract true intimacy and connection.

As you reenter the dating scene, I challenge you to do so *without* your armor, with an open heart, and with the recognition that if you want someone to love you in a different way this time around, you need to love yourself in a more intimate, vulnerable, and authentic way first. You can't form a strong new bond with someone without being vulnerable. Opening your heart to love again is the most vulnerable thing you can do since there's always the possibility of getting hurt. It's a risk. At times it may feel safer to swear off men and become a scorned ice queen with a frozen heart, but that'll only perpetuate feeling alone and flawed. Author Madeleine L'Engle nails it when she says, "When we were children, we used to think that when we were grown-up we would no longer be vulnerable. But to grow up is to accept vulnerability . . . . To be alive is to be vulnerable." Love gives us purpose and meaning. Your heartbreak was full of shame, fear, and a struggle for worthiness; you were stripped down and forced to be painfully raw and vulnerable with yourself. But to receive the love and belonging that you deeply desire, you must also stand fiercely in your vulnerability. Rather than be scared of it, reframe vulnerability as a sign of strength. You are braver and stronger than you realize.

EXERCISE: VULNERABILITY BREATHING

Let's do a quick mindfulness breathing exercise around vulnerability.

> **Step 1**: Sit in a comfortable position, allowing your body to be supported in a chair and relaxing your muscles. Close your eyes and begin breathing in through your nose and out through your mouth at a steady pace.

> **Step 2**: Bring your attention to the protective wall you've built that prevents you from being vulnerable. Envision yourself wearing a heavy coat of armor.

> **Step 3**: Imagine taking off the armor, piece by piece, starting with your helmet, moving down to your chest plate, shoulder guards, and so on until you've removed every heavy piece down to your toes, standing naked and free. Though you are exposed, you feel powerful.

Step 4: Now that the armor has been removed, with every deep in breath, breathe in joy, belonging, and love. Feel your body fill up with the warmth of these words. With every out breath, breathe out any remaining shame, fear, and unworthiness. Feel your body lighten as you release this toxic energy. Continue breathing in joy, belonging, and love and exhaling shame, fear, and unworthiness until your mind, body, and heart feels totally open and exposed.

Step 5: You are now free to embrace vulnerability and welcome love into your life. To end the meditation, say out loud, "I embrace vulnerability, and I welcome love into my life."

Now that you're fully able to embrace vulnerability, let's tackle some other important dating mind-sets so that you can set realistic expectations for this next step in your bounce-back journey.

REALISTIC DATING MIND-SETS

Don't let every micro-rejection bruise your ego. Micro-rejections are the small but many ways in which your interest and affection may not be returned. It could be the hottie on Tinder that didn't swipe right, the unanswered message on Bumble after you've had some promising back-and-forths, getting stood up or canceled on last minute, or being ghosted after a date that could not have gone better. No one likes getting rejected, but it's part of dating.

Dating is both a personal and impersonal experience. When you walk down the street, are you attracted to everyone you pass by? No, of course not! And not all of them are attracted to you either, and that's okay. We all have our own preferences, and these won't always match up. If you can approach dating with the mind-set that not everyone will like you or be your future husband, then you can accept the disappointments and continue dating until you find a great partner with reciprocal feelings. Not being a match is actually a blessing in disguise because it means you can stop investing and find someone who is. We have to not take it personally when we aren't a match and focus on the process instead.

You will have some bad dates. You might go on some disaster dates, but those will be funny stories to laugh about with friends. You'll likely shed some tears along the way too, but to be resilient you need to laugh and smile your way through this process, rather than approach it with dread and cynicism. Worst-case scenario is that you waste an evening that could have been better spent meeting someone else. Dating duds just help to clarify what exactly you like and what works for you. So even if they're not Prince Charming, they're a human and dating is likely difficult for them too, so be kind.

Dating is casual until it's committed. The whole point of dating is to meet and get to know someone to see if there's chemistry and attraction. It's figuring out if you have shared life goals, core values, and complementary personality traits. You should only commit to someone when they fall high on your ideal match scale.

You have the power to choose. If you're not rejecting anyone, there's a good chance you're not dating with intent. Instead, you might be waiting for someone to pick you or validate you, in which case your armor is back on. Dating isn't about sitting around passively waiting to be liked, or changing yourself for someone else's approval. You're not a chameleon that should change your colors based on who you are dating. A rewarding dating life stems from knowing who you are and what you want, and not compromising on your deal breakers. You can take control of your dating life by realizing it's not so much about whether they like you, but whether you like them, and you have the power to reject someone too. You will find your ideal match when you show up authentically and vulnerably in the process, which means there's no room for your dating defenses.

You can't make someone love you, but you can control the type of love you're willing to receive and accept. When you've done the work on yourself and can ditch your dating defenses and show up authentically and vulnerably, you'll lose your taste for those who can't do the same. If you're used to dating emotionally unavailable partners, a good rule of thumb is to mirror the energy and effort they put forward in the early stages so that you don't invest too much. You'll know pretty quickly whether they're as open for love as you are. When you value yourself and own your worth, you stop wasting your time trying to get someone to love you, to give you attention, to make you a priority, and you focus your attention only on those that show up ready, willing, and able to meet your needs. You can't make someone love you, but you can control the type of love you're willing to receive and accept.

No one can predict when you'll meet your ideal match, so you just have to keep dating until you do. The more you analyze your dating data and learn from your love lessons, the more deliberate you can be about the partners you choose to commit to, minimizing unnecessary breakups. Minimize dating stress by refusing to operate your life from an artificial timeline.

Manage dating disappointments with optimism. Rather than beat yourself up with nonsense, such as "I'll never find someone," "Something's wrong with me," or "I'm going to die alone," speak to yourself with compassion and positivity. How about, "I know my ideal match is out there. I'm ready to receive love and create connection" or, "I'm proud that I'm putting myself out there." Instead of approaching dating as a means to get to an end, be present and enjoy the process along the way—from getting dressed up to learning about the person sitting across from you.

Think of your first few dates as practice rounds. Don't psych yourself out before you've even gotten out there. Instead of worrying about the outcome of the date, focus on showing up confident and secure, without your armor, practicing vulnerability, and presenting your authentic self, which is a big win, even if you don't go on a second date. Thinking or assuming he's your future husband before your first date, or after just one meeting, doesn't serve you and leads to unrealistic expectations. Your job isn't to fall in love with the *idea* of them, but the real version of them. On a first date your main goal should be figuring out if there's enough chemistry and common interests or shared visions to warrant a second date.

YOUR BRAIN ON A DATE

When my client Jackie first came to me, I learned that she'd been "fibbing" on her dates in an attempt to impress them. She'd grossly exaggerate about the hobbies she was into, or change her opinions about seemingly unimportant topics to pique their interest and form a connection. She said this wasn't intentional, but she'd be so nervous and excited on the first date that she'd inadvertently say whatever she thought they wanted to hear.

Let's look at what was going on in Jackie's brain so that you can be a little more empathetic to her fibbing behavior. Your brain is in charge of the ways you perceive and respond to stimuli. In *Wired for Love*, Dr. Stan Tatkin calls the parts of your brain designed to keep you alive and safe your "primitives," which act quickly and automatically. Other parts of the brain act as "ambassadors," correcting errors made by the primitives. The ambassadors provide social restraints that allow us to interact appropriately with others. In his other book, *Wired for Dating*, Dr. Tatkin describes how when you first meet someone you scan the stranger and environment for signs of danger. In order to keep you safe, your amygdala, a primitive brain mechanism, constantly assesses for dangerous behaviors, faces, or words. If it detects any of these, it acts as an alarm system that activates the stress response and your innate reaction is to fight, flee, or even freeze. Talk about how awkward that would be on a first date to dash out the door, attack your date, or fumble for words! So in order to not look like a total weirdo, your brain has to cope with this alarm system and that's where the more rational ambassadors come into play.

Let's say Jackie tells her date that her idea of a perfect Sunday morning is sleeping in and going out for a Bloody Mary. She's expecting him to smile and agree, but her amygdala processes that the corners of his mouth droop downwards into a frown and his eyes narrow. Her primitives quickly pick up on his unenthusiastic response and the danger alarm goes off. Your primitives aren't designed to figure out why he's frowning, it just notifies you that you might be in danger of being embarrassed or rejected. But don't worry, ambassadors (anterior cingulate and orbital frontal cortex) to the rescue! These brain regions jump in to correct mistakes that the primitives make. Jackie's ambassadors quickly identify possible causes for his reaction—"Does he think I'm lazy?" "Do I sound like a lush?"—then they rattle off advice: "Quick, change the topic!"

Dr. Tatkin points out that your ambassadors keep working trying to predict your next social mistake, which keeps your primitives engaged, since they are heightened for trouble. That means our brain is using a lot of energy to make sure we're safe and don't make social blunders. This back-and-forth loop between our ambassadors and primitives is what's known as performance anxiety, which we can call first date anxiety. This first date anxiety can be accompanied by symptoms such as blushing, nausea, shaking, racing heart, sweating, or feeling faint. Knowing we have some of these embarrassing symptoms can also take up our conscious thoughts; worrying we might have armpit sweat stains—ugh! Because Jackie's mental energy is caught up in this loop, she's not totally comfortable being herself. In fact, because she's hyperaware of all of her date's nonverbal behaviors, she starts responding in ways that receive a favorable response. This is when Jackie gets into trouble because in order to feel less foolish she'll redirect with a comment such as, "I'm just kidding, I usually wake up early and go for a run." This fib will gain his approval and get the date back on track, and ultimately avoid embarrassment. The problem with this is that Jackie isn't being authentic. The health-conscious guy in front of her is hoping to meet a gal who'll hit up a 6:00 a.m. CrossFit class with him, and it only takes him a few weeks into dating Jackie to discover she much prefers 11:00 a.m. brunch.

Now that you're aware of how your primitives and ambassadors interact, you can be more mindful and aware of *false advertisement*. If you misrepresent who you are, dates who aren't an ideal match will pursue you based on the image you're presenting. The buyer (aka your potential partner) will then be disappointed that you don't perform as advertised, and return you to the dating market. To prevent this, you have to consciously manage that anxiety feedback loop, and remind your brain that you're not in actual danger. Simple ways to keep your body and brain calm and collected are to take deep breaths before talking, drink water, and even push up your sleeves to cool off. These actions soothe your body and regulate your heart rate so that you feel calmer. As long as your date isn't an axe murderer, in which case your brain's alert to danger is legit and you need to get the f*$k out, the only danger is them not wanting to go on another date. You can live with that. Rather than bait them with false advertisement, don't autocorrect yourself with a falsified, favorable response. The right partner will fit comfortably into your life, and the best way to figure that out is by being authentically you. Remember Brené Brown's definition of belonging? She said that because of our primal need for belonging, we try to acquire it by fitting in and seeking approval. Fitting in is about *changing* who you are to gain acceptance, whereas belonging is *being* who you are. Stay true to you.

Today and every day moving forward, I want you to practice living authentically and embracing vulnerability, even when you're scared or it feels easier to hide or self-sabotage. Commit to a daily intention-setting practice to shift your mood and energy. Wake up and say out loud the following statement:

> *Today I choose to lower my defenses,*
> *to love myself, and*
> *to see myself as worthy.*
> *I choose to show up vulnerably so that*
> *I can attract and receive the love*
> *that I deserve.*

SECTION 3

Life beyond Breakup

Time for a quick recap. When you can check these off, you'll be saying bye-bye breakup:

✓ I'm practicing self-love daily.

✓ I have recognized my inner voice and am learning how to trust my intuition.

✓ I am feeling more confident, am setting higher standards for how I want to be treated, and know what I deserve in a future relationship.

✓ I have challenged my fears and negative beliefs about dating, and am operating from a mind-set of hope and abundance.

✓ I am making a conscious effort to live and date with authenticity and vulnerability.

CHAPTER 14

Your Ideal Match

The most exciting aspect about your breakup is that it's a chance for a fresh start. You no longer need to settle. No more abusers, cheaters, someone unsupportive, someone who makes you feel small, someone who devalues you, someone who doesn't prioritize your needs, or someone who doesn't bother to acknowledge your unhappiness. Instead, you get to dream up your ideal match, and then go meet them in real life. When you believe you're worthy and operate from a mind-set of abundance, such as "I know I'm a catch and I can't wait to meet the many men who value the same things I do, and will treat me with kindness and respect," then the world is your dating playground. You deserve someone who makes you feel like the most attractive, enchanting, and valuable woman on the planet. My husband told me on our third date that when he's with me he sees stars (he even had a star named after me for a Valentine's Day gift). Romance does exist, and so does a profound, reciprocal love after a breakup. Your unicorn is out there too!

But before we go any further in discussing your ideal match, we need to address the elephant in the room—no, you're not shallow for caring about looks! You just need to make sure there's something underneath them to back up the attraction. Certain evolutionary factors drive us toward picking an attractive partner. For instance, we prefer tall people with symmetrical faces because it signals they're healthy, and since our innate drive is to pick a mating partner, it makes sense we'd want someone with good genes. It

155

takes less than one second to determine if we're attracted to someone. This is probably why hot-or-not-style dating apps became so wildly popular—not because they're promoting quality matches based on mutual interests and shared values, but because it only takes one second to make a judgment, swipe right or left and receive instant gratification.

While physical attraction alone is a bad metric for a relationship, it does need to be in the mix. Sometimes we can find someone great on paper, but the attraction falls flat in person. They're too short, you hate the dark black pores on their nose, or they smell funny. As much as I want you to keep an open mind, you can't force yourself to be attracted to someone. Ask yourself, "Can I see past what's turning me off?" Beards can be trimmed, cologne can be purchased, and bald guys can be phenomenal kissers. Ultimately though, no matter how many dates you give them, if you can't develop that spark and sexual attraction the relationship is a no-go. When I was actively online dating there was a man whose profile looked like my perfect match, but I wasn't attracted to his photos. He continued to send me hilarious messages, and eventually I caved and messaged back because he was so funny. Despite the fact that he was an athletic, intelligent, successful doctor holding a giant bouquet and tickets to the Red Sox game for our first date, the second I saw him in person I knew in my gut that I wasn't attracted to him. I tried to keep an open mind, and even gave him three dates since we had great convos, a lot of shared values, and he made me laugh; but every time I'd open my door to greet him I could feel my heart sink. When he went in for the first kiss, I cringed and crossed my fingers for fireworks, but all I could think about was how much I hated the feeling of his thin lips pressed against mine. I ended it then.

IDEAL MATCH THEORY

I'm going to let you in on my personal theory, but don't worry, I won't go all Einstein on you! You don't need a degree in science or psychology to understand it and apply it to your life. This is my theory about love. It's called the *Ideal Match Theory*. I believe that every partner falls on a scale from 1 to 100, with 100 being your most well-suited, complementary match. If you're with your ideal match, your personalities are complementary; your core values are aligned; you have a secure functioning relationship full of safety, trust, intimacy, and effective communication; you know how to soothe each other and repair conflict; you tackle problems and approach life as a unified team; you speak each other's love languages and prioritize each other consistently; and of course there is physical attraction and sexual compatibility. You don't have to enjoy all of the same activities together, but you do have to agree on how much time you like to spend together versus your need for independence. Your ideal match isn't a clone; you value and respect each other's differences. It's kind of like in *Sex and the City* when Samantha asked Charlotte how often she's happy in her relationship, and Charlotte replied that with Harry she's happy every day. Not all day every day, but at least daily.

Even after you've been with your ideal match for years, you still feel enamored, continue to grow a deeper sense of connection, and cultivate a truly meaningful partnership. This wild love is not one of myth; it exists in real life. Dr. Helen Fisher studied couples who reported being madly in love after on average twenty-one years of marriage. She and a team of researchers wanted to know what made these couples different and how they could sustain feelings of deep love for each other over such a long period of time. She put these couples into a brain scanner, and found three distinct regions of brain activity.

The first brain region is associated with *empathy*. Empathy is the ability to put yourself in your partner's shoes and understand their own emotional experiences. It's saying, "When you're distraught, the world stops and I will listen and feel with you." It's being on the same team instead of against each other. These long-term lovers can relieve each other's pain. A relationship cannot survive without empathy. One of the most helpful skill sets in any relationship is effective communication, which is directly correlated with having empathetic regard for your partner.

I teach my clients my **L.U.V.E.** acronym, which stands for *listen, understand, validate,* and *empathize*. To listen, you must give your partner your full attention, and show this by putting your phone down, making eye contact, and nodding along. To understand, you should repeat back or paraphrase to your partner what you just heard them say, which gives your partner a chance to clarify anything and feel that you really get the core of the issue. You can combine validate and empathize into the final step, which is to make a validating and empathetic response, such as, "I can see why that would be frustrating or why you would be hurt," which shows your partner that you can relate to their emotional experience. Note that I didn't say you have to agree with your partner or that it's about right and wrong, rather it's about stepping into your partner's emotional reality.

The second brain region pinpointed by the research is associated with *controlling your own emotions*. To stay in love for so long, you must be responsible for your own emotional reactions and take responsibility for your behaviors, no matter how angry or annoyed you are. Even couples therapists, like me, make mistakes. There have been times I've caught myself yelling at my husband, saying, "Why did *you* make me yell?" as if he could reach into my throat and control my own vocal cords! I will never be perfect, but I can recognize these unfair accusations and apologize for them. Owning your emotional reactions rather than blaming them on your partner is key to creating a relationship in which there is trust, respect, and accountability.

The skill here is about being able to self-regulate. When you're angry or upset, the fight-or-flight region of your brain is activated, and this can prevent you from accessing the more rational, decision-making part of your brain. When you feel yourself escalating, a good technique is to take your internal temperature. Ask yourself where you fall on a 1 to 10 scale. If it's above a 5, it means you're probably not thinking logically, and you may say or do something that will hurt your partner. Of course, if you're already above a 5, it may be too late to do this rationale exercise, so it takes practice to check in with yourself as you feel yourself starting to heat up. This is the best time to take three long, deep breaths, and tell your partner that you need to take a short time-out to cool off so that you can have a more productive conversation. Make sure to tell your partner that you know this is important to them, and you intend to finish the discussion. Otherwise, they'll think you're blowing them off.

The third brain region that lit up in the brain scanner is an area associated with what Dr. Fisher calls *positive illusions*, which is the ability to overlook what you don't like about your partner and hyper-focus on what you do like. This may seem like a super-power, but with a daily practice of gratitude (there's that word again!), you can have this skill too. Gratitude can help you focus on what you love and cherish, and when we bring this to the forefront of our mind, all the other annoyances won't seem as significant. Every night, I want you and your partner to create a gratitude tradition where you appreciate one thoughtful thing that your partner did that day. It should be small and specific, such as loading the dishes in the dishwasher, or the "I miss you" text they sent while at work. Not only does it feel really wonderful to be genuinely appreciated by your partner, but you'll notice it quickly begins to change your own behavior, since you're going out of your way to do something nice for your partner. This gratitude practice can change the entire dynamic in your relationship as you begin to be more mindful of your own actions and the ways in which your partner shows you love. Building on the gratitude practice, there's actually a magic ratio of 5:1 that Dr. John Gottman, a world-renowned couples researcher, identified in which there must be five positive interactions for every negative one. Saying five nice things to your partner daily reduces their cortisol and cholesterol levels and boosts their immune system. So, in deciding whether or not to comment on what's bugging you, make sure you've given your partner plenty of compliments and affection first to balance out the criticism. The couples in this study are a prime example of #relationshipgoals and have abilities we should all strive toward.

Couples who don't align on everything can absolutely make their relationship work, but they must accept that they can't change the things they don't like about their partners. There must be a shift away from defining the relationship by what's lacking. An ideal match is the perfect partner for you, but is *not* a perfect person; those don't exist. *Every* potential partner will have quirks and qualities that get under your skin or that you'll bicker over; that's called being human, so you need to adjust your expectations. One consistent trait of all humans is that we are imperfect; we make mistakes, we act out, we do and say hurtful things, we put ourselves first, we struggle. A relationship is a team made up of two people, therefore it's inherently imperfect. When you're with your ideal match it doesn't mean that you'll never have a disagreement or that there will be passionate romance 24–7. Finding your ideal match is all about knowing yourself and picking a teammate who complements you in certain areas and balances you in others. You're striving for the yin to your yang, which does not require either partner to be perfect.

For the perfectionists out there, it's not about saying, "I found a 90 percent match, but I can do better so I need to find my 100 percent match." Instead, it's first and foremost about whether you feel happy the majority of the time. Then, if you've determined that the non-ideals aren't deal breakers, reflect on whether you're dissatisfied because it feels like settling versus just being part of a team of two imperfect humans. If the goal is perfection, date a robot and good luck getting your emotional needs met! The reason you want to join a team is because the whole is greater than the sum of the parts—our old friend Aristotle was onto something. Can you let go of your partner's "flaws," which aren't actually flaws, but rather qualities and traits that aren't in alignment with yours or different than your definition of ideal or how you choose to do something? When you choose to overlook and accept what you don't like, and love them as they are, you can be really happy.

Here are some baseline descriptors for the ideal match scale:

IDEAL MATCH SCALE

100: Soul mate status, you're two peas in a pod.

90–99: Every day you have grateful and blissful moments.

80–89: You feel connected and generally happy, though a couple of your needs may be unmet.

70–79: Satisfied sometimes, but you question if there's a better fit out there, since not all of your core values align and your personality traits bump heads.

60–69: You argue frequently or wish you could change major things about your partner.

50–59: You often feel disconnected and have seriously contemplated ending the relationship.

40–49: You have hot sex and share a fun hobby, but that's about it.

30–39: You probably should not have gone past the first date.

0–29: You deserve better and have some serious soul-searching to do around self-worth and self-esteem.

Actual love, as in unconditional love, doesn't mean you love everything about the person. It means you don't need them to be different than they are for you to be happy.

AUTHOR UNKNOWN

EXERCISE: REFLECTING ON YOUR IDEAL MATCH SCORE

In your Bounce Back Journal write down where you rate your ex on the scale. Reflect on the following questions:

- ♥ How do you feel about the score? Does it feel acceptable, or as though you settled or compromised too much?

- ♥ What would've you needed to be different in the relationship in order to give your ex a score that's ten points closer to an ideal match?

- ♥ What, if any, were the things you tried to accept about your ex that were actually deal breakers?

- ♥ Why did you compromise on your deal breakers?

- ♥ What qualities will your future ideal match have (notice I did not ask you to describe their physical appearance)?

Your ex was *not* your ideal match. You wouldn't be in this situation if they were. They may have been good enough at the time, but ultimately what was missing or broken led to the end of the relationship. Zoom out from your current pain to focus on the bigger picture of what you want for yourself and your love life, and repeat after me: "I can do better, I will pick smarter." This heartbreak is leading you in a positive direction, toward the possibility of an ideal match.

There are some things in life worth settling for, like a vanilla cupcake when the chocolate lava fudge is sold out, but we're talking about your love life here! Sometimes people choose a partner lower on the scale because they're in love and unwilling to let go even though it's not the best match, they struggle with low self-esteem and have felt unlovable their entire lives, or settle for a status "quople" relationship because they fear being alone. I get it. It's hard to feel hopeful about your love life when your future partner looks like a giant question mark and doesn't exist in your life yet. It's a leap of faith—faith in yourself that you deserve more and can achieve it.

Just because your ex was a good fish, doesn't mean they're your best catch. I know it's hard to let them swim away, but it's time to focus on reeling in a better catch for you. Take some time to recuperate on the shore (I mean that figuratively, but doesn't a postbreakup beach vacay sound great right about now?), and then get back out there in your fishing boat. You may want to cast a wide net and be open to many new dating experiences if you're still in the process of figuring out the qualities of an ideal catch, or hook a specific type of fish now that you have more clarity about what you want. We'll talk about the most important things to look for in a partner in chapter 15.

DEAL BREAKERS

A deal breaker is a fundamental belief, personality trait, or core value that you cannot compromise on and that conflicts with the belief or lifestyle of your partner. An easy example is knowing for a fact that you want to have kids and dating someone who does not. This significantly violates the way in which you want to live your life, and is something important that you should not compromise on. Only you can define your deal breakers. For example, after a long-standing unhealthy relationship with herself and, by extension, the men she welcomed into her life, my dear friend Catherine decided to start loving herself, and therefore set higher standards for the love she was willing to accept from others. She knew she could only be with someone who had a strong sense of spirituality, so she'd ask potential partners whether they believed in God on their first date, and cut them loose if they didn't share this value. She and her now-husband connected on their spiritual beliefs on their first date.

Deal breakers shouldn't be trivial issues, such as how your partner chews their food or hating the emoji they insert at the end of their texts. In total honesty here, I was really turned off when my husband and I were first getting to know each other and he texted me "Sweet dreamz :-)" Ugh. I stared at that "z" and ugly smiley face and questioned if this was really the guy I was meant to be with. Imagine if I'd ended it right there, what a monumental mistake that would've been. This was *not* a deal breaker. I also used to get really annoyed that he's messy and doesn't clean up after himself (I'm also guilty of doing the exact same thing, so perhaps I'm projecting here), but the point is that although this issue isn't ideal, it doesn't violate the ways in which I need to live my life. Would I like my house to be a little more organized? Sure, but it's not one of my core values, so I had to consciously put this issue in the accept bucket when I picked him as my life partner. There are some nights I have to consciously choose to overlook the sink piled up with dishes and focus on what I love and appreciate about him.

It's up to *you* to define your deal breakers and decide if you can accept your new partner as is without compromising on your core values. When trying to figure out what differences and grievances you can accept, ask yourself if it conflicts with the vision you have for your life. Can you be flexible on this issue, or is it unwavering? How does it impact you? Does it play into your shame story and validate your old framework of emotional injuries that you're trying to rewrite? Will you feel like you're not honoring your own values and needs by compromising and accepting your partner's way of doing things? As you know, compromise is an important skill required to be in a relationship. At times you'll need to put your partner's wants first. Yet, there's a big difference between compromising on where to eat dinner or what movie to watch than dating someone who loves trophy hunting when you're an animal rights activist. When we're talking about core values, "settling" is a breeding ground for resentment. Do some soul-searching and hold steadfast to what's most important to you.

Just because I use the phrase "ideal match," doesn't mean there's only one possible person out there for you. An ideal match is someone who makes you feel the most like yourself. I believe you can be an ideal match with multiple people, since there are a ton of fabulous options out there in the world. You have to be an expert on yourself to be able to snag that special someone. Your core values may shift over time with life experience, or through your dating experiences something may become more or less important to you. You can't recognize an ideal match until you know and understand yourself. By dating with intent, you can figure out where each date falls on your own ideal match scale.

I want your experience in picking a partner to be an active, conscious decision, instead of something you fall into. The worst thing you can do is be impulsive about the process. For instance, let's pretend you're at the mall and see a pair of stunning stilettos with sky-high heels. You snatch them up immediately; you've always wanted a pair like these. You fantasize about all of the times you'll wear them, how fantastic they'll look on you and how they'll make you feel like a rock star. You make a quick impulse purchase. But once you get home and put them on, you realize how inflexible and uncomfortable they are. They don't provide enough support and keep rubbing you the wrong way. You start to blister, but continue to wear them because you love them and you paid a lot for them. You're hoping to break them in to fit your foot, but you realize they'll never fit exactly the way you want them to. This is like impulsively choosing a partner because of intense physical attraction and chemistry, or a fantasy of how you'd be together, even though in reality they're not as comfortable and seamless a fit as expected. They could be a wonderful shoe, but if you choose wrong, you'll wind up hurt with emotional blisters.

I don't want to create a black-and-white rule by giving you a number on the ideal match scale and telling you to never remain in a partnership with someone who falls below a circumscribed number. You need to identify that number for yourself. Where are your standards? Do they reflect the best version of you; the one in which you love yourself and honor your values? Each relationship will have its own unique set of challenges; however, what I'm trying to hit home is that with the right partner you'll feel like you're winning at love because of everything that an ideal match represents. Make the most of your fresh start. When you honor the best version of yourself, you won't put up with anyone low on your scale.

As if you don't have enough to consider, I'm going to throw one more large, mind-blowing concept at you. When I talk about core values, a good portion of that is *nurture*, not *nature*. Your background—how you were raised, your culture and ethnicity, socioeconomic status, interpersonal relationships—has a big impact on your values and lifestyle. But even when you're handed a partner who checks off all of these boxes, sometimes you're still not attracted to them. So what's missing? It's important that we don't ignore nature, our biological underpinnings. Our traits of temperament are linked to certain genes, hormones, and neurotransmitter systems, and thanks to science and technology we now know that they play a big role in our love lives. Dr. Helen Fisher's extensive research has led her to identify four personality types that correlate with attraction and who we choose to love. Basically, nature plays a significant role too.

According to Fisher, we each have a primary and secondary type of thinking and behaving that guides us in choosing a romantic partner. Roughly 50 percent of the variations in our personality are due to biology, which are heritable and stable throughout our life. Fisher developed the Fisher Temperament Inventory, and assessed responses from over one hundred thousand singles, as well as conducted brain scan studies to determine that the four brain systems (based on the hormones dopamine, serotonin, testosterone, and estrogen) are associated with different personality types. Let's look briefly at the four different types, but I highly recommend you read Fisher's book *Why Him? Why Her?* and take the test yourself so that you can more thoroughly learn about your type and who you might be attracted to. It's simply fascinating. For instance, have you ever heard the saying "opposites attract"? Fisher found this to be true, but just for two of the four types, which I've noted below:

> **Explorers (dopamine):** curious, energetic, spontaneous, impulsive, novelty-seeking, creative, self-reliant, and sexual. Explorers tend to be drawn to other Explorers, who are animated and energetic and likely have an expressive face. They seek an entertaining playmate, and can find self-disclosure difficult, so they deflect with humor.

> **Builders (serotonin):** traditional, calm, cautious, persistent, literal, loyal, social, managerial, cooperative, respectful, and modest. Builders tend to be drawn to other Builders, and are attracted to someone who looks more conservative, with less makeup and a traditional haircut. They have clear values, are dependable, have good manners, and like to keep a schedule. Builders seek a help-mate, someone stable, predictable, and a team player. They like to be social and are community-oriented.

> **Directors (testosterone):** competitive, direct, tough-minded, bold, focused, inventive, decisive, analytical, and strategic. Directors are more frequently men (but Hillary Clinton is a good example of a female Director), with a take-charge attitude. They tend to have angular faces, chiseled jaws, wide shoulders, and a deep voice.

Directors do best with Negotiators. They're attracted to a mind mate, someone with a similar intellect and shared goals, who is more social and emotionally expressive.

Negotiators (estrogen): empathetic, imaginative, trusting, emotionally expressive, affectionate, agreeable, introspective, loquacious, and intuitive. They tend to have big eyes, a round face, and full lips. Negotiators do best with Directors, and they crave a deep personal connection. They seek the intimacy of a soul mate and work hard to promote harmony in a relationship. Negotiators may be the most deeply hurt by rejection.

The way you find love after a breakup may even be unique to your personality type—something to consider as you bounce back. Fisher posits that Explorers thrive on change and novel situations in which they're optimistic and flexible, leading them to notice new people. Builders like stability, so they may seek out a new partner during this stressful time. Directors like to feel useful and needed, so they help others around them and may stumble upon new love. Negotiators become anxious, so they reach out to others to build deep connections.

As you begin to date again, it's important to recognize that although you may share many core values with a new suitor, you could have conflicting personality traits that may impair your connection and ultimately lead to the downfall of your relationship. We'll share core values with many people, but they can't all be an ideal match for us even so. Use this information to create the best partnership possible for you.

You deserve more than to settle when you're unhappy or when there are significant value or personality differences that cause chronic problems. Major signs you're not dating your ideal match are if you don't like yourself in the relationship, or if you're constantly criticizing your partner and hoping they will change. My mother, the wisest woman I know, once told me that you should be with the person that you want to change the least. I'll say that again, since I just dropped a serious wisdom bomb: *Be with the person that you want to change the least.* It takes life experience to realize the value in this statement. That's because when you've only dated one or two people, you have nothing to compare it to, and you may try to force a relationship to work that would be best to leave. It's difficult to figure out if you're being too demanding, what your values are, and whether you're compromising too much, especially if you allow your old destructive assumptions and negative internalized beliefs to rule your dating choices. The good thing is you're no longer going to sell yourself short. With the increased self-awareness and insight you've gained and your new adult narrative that you're worthy and deserving of love, you're going to firmly label your deal breakers so that you don't minimize your wants, needs, goals, and values. Your more ideal match is out there.

CHAPTER 15

Core Values and Relationship Requirements in Intentional Dating

I'm in the business of helping people find and create lasting love, so if you're looking for a serious relationship with long-term potential, this chapter is going to be key. Dating with purpose first requires you to have a clear sense of who you are and what's most important to you so that you can align these needs and values with another to create an ideal match. Going on multiple dates with the same person should become an increasingly intentional process of learning about their belief systems and core values. Of course you still want to have flirtation and fun; it's not an interview and you're not grilling them, but it should be an enjoyable experience where you're both exploring each other mentally, spiritually, emotionally, and yes, physically too. When I say exploring, forget all of the rules you've learned about when to talk about what. It's no longer a dating faux pas to get into contentious subjects, like religion or politics, up front. The 2016 *Singles in America* survey conducted annually by Match.com examined over 5,500 American singles from around the country, ages eighteen to over seventy, and found that 80 percent of singles think talking about politics, money, and religion are fair game. In fact, the survey found that discussing political issues increases your chances of getting a second date by 91 percent, 25 percent of singles say not being registered to vote is an instant deal breaker, and 35 percent will not consider dating someone who doesn't have an opinion on key political issues. This tells us singles want to be talking about what matters most to them.

KEEP AN OPEN MIND

Relationships can develop at different paces. This is especially true for people dating with different attachment styles, so realize that your romantic passions can grow with time. Not all successful relationships start off with fireworks, even when you're physically attracted to each other. Some relationships develop from friendships, and in fact a study found that valuing friendship with your partner creates relationships with more commitment, love, and greater sexual satisfaction. Thanks to social psychologist Leon Festinger and the proximity principle, we know that we tend to develop stronger relationships with those people we're around more frequently. That means the more you see someone, the more you may like them. If you're on the fence, do yourself a favor and give someone that has potential the benefit of the doubt, and go on the extra date with them.

If you're struggling to develop a deeper connection, but suspect there's underlying qualities that make them a keeper, ask yourself how would someone with a secure attachment feel, act, and behave? To boost intimacy, you can try a few things. First, ask increasingly intimate questions (see core value questions to ask a partner below). Observing how a date responds to certain questions like these, such as if they dodge them or fail to go beneath the surface, may give you insight into their level of comfort with closeness. Do they laugh it off, brush it off, or expect you to answer each question first before sharing their own opinion? It's a good indication that someone has a secure attachment or at least is presenting authentically and vulnerably if they can engage and expand upon these conversations, exploring their own responses in addition to yours. Also make sure to make a lot of eye contact. Research found prolonged eye contact synchronizes brain activity between two people and connects them with shared attention, so this can elevate your connection. Lastly, make physical contact. You're looking for a romantic relationship, not just a friendship, so it's imperative to break the touch barrier and see how you feel in each other's arms. Hugging, kissing,

Love is friendship that has caught fire. It is quiet understanding, mutual confidence, sharing, and forgiving. It is loyalty through good and bad times. It settles for less than perfection and makes allowances for human weaknesses.

ANN LANDERS

touching someone's arm, or holding hands can decrease the stress hormone cortisol; and touch that lasts at least twenty seconds releases oxytocin, which can stimulate feelings of trust, bonding, and devotion. Experiencing this canoodling can make you feel closer to a new partner.

CORE VALUES

Core values can seem a bit abstract, so I'll break some down for you shortly with big-ticket items to contemplate. It may feel overwhelming to review this list, but there's no pressure to answer everything at once. That said, your dating journey will be so much easier if you have clarity on these questions. Oftentimes, we make the mistake of committing before we really discuss core values. You begin casually seeing someone and by the time your core values become an issue or cause conflict in your relationship, you've already invested love, time, and energy, so you're less likely to really question if this is the best fit for you. Before you know it, poof, you're a status "quople"! You can't know who's an ideal match for you before you know what you value most. For example, maybe you've always been environmentally conscious, but didn't identify this as a core value until you dated a guy who didn't recycle or care about his carbon footprint. During your dating journey, many of these values will become clear deal breakers on which you should never compromise. As time passes, you may find your preferences and what's most crucial may shift. That's okay as long as you're self-aware and take time to ask yourself which values guide the way you want to live your life. Collecting this dating data will help you identify a partner who could be an ideal match, instead of settling with someone because of extreme physical attraction or superficial qualities. Superficial qualities are typically things such as enjoying the same food, music, or sports, or sharing a friend group. That said, for some people food choices may reflect deeper core values, such as living a health-conscious lifestyle, or being a vegetarian to stand against animal cruelty. Only you can define your core values, so be mindful about why you're ruling a potential partner in or out. Be aware we all have values, but not all our values are our core values, which are those that are most important to us.

Also, look out for the *paper champion*, especially with online dating. It's easy to be fooled by someone who checks off all of your superficial boxes—tall, dark, handsome, super-successful surgeon, hotshot lawyer, professional athlete. With a paper champion, the attraction is all about their achievements instead of their core values and personality traits. You may be drawn to this unconsciously, in an attempt to cover up your own underlying wounds and insecurities, seeking worthiness through association. That's why I've asked you to do so much work on yourself so that you can catch these dynamics and choose smarter.

Sometimes we're drawn to someone because of an electric physical spark, which can deceive you into thinking there's a stronger connection than what really exists. In this case, you're likely getting swept away by the love potion. Let's take a time-out to talk about how love, lust, and attraction impact you on a neuropsychological level. When you develop a crush on someone, your brain produces a neurochemical cocktail of hormones and chemicals that give you that excited, anxious, jittery, attached, and hyper-focused feeling. The big players are dopamine, testosterone, estrogen, oxytocin, vasopressin, noradrenaline, and serotonin. Even when you just think of your crush, your brain releases the feel-good neurotransmitter dopamine, responsible for euphoria, cravings, and obsessive focus. The surge of excitement and nerves when you're first hanging out is due to the chemicals adrenaline and norepinephrine, which is also responsible for infatuated thinking. As you now know, love is addicting, so the limbic system is activated and keeps you coming back for more, while your amygdala takes a nap so you're less judgmental and might overlook red flags. Then in comes oxytocin, nicknamed the "cuddle hormone" which is released during skin-to-skin physical touch and during an orgasm. Oxytocin creates trust, commitment, and attachment. You might mistake this love potion as a magnetic connection signaling true compatibility. This is one of the reasons I encourage singles to get to know each other first with quality, in-depth conversation before hopping into the sack. Good sex can confuse things and make it harder to figure out if your feelings are so strong because of the love potion, or because you really like each other. In this early, passionate stage, you're more likely to overlook red flags and compromise deal breakers because you're so smitten.

Aligning core values isn't the most romantic approach to finding love, but it's practical and can set you up for success in the long run. That's because long-lasting love is multi-faceted, with elements of passion and attraction; companionship and deep affection; flirtation and novelty; sacrifice and kindness; and shared values and goals. Review the following list, taking notes in your Bounce Back Journal as you explore your own beliefs, as well as the core values you ideally want in a partner.

CORE VALUES TO CONSIDER

- ♥ How do you define the concept of a family? Is your family important to you? How much do you want them involved in your life? How frequently do you like to spend time with your family? Do your family members have a lot of influence over your life decisions?

- ♥ How do you feel about having children? What are your beliefs about parenting? Do you imagine your children having a similar upbringing as you?

- ♥ How important is culture and race to your personal identity? Is it important to you that you date someone with the same culture and race? What issues do you have dating someone from a different culture or race?

- ♥ Do you value education and learning? What degree do you have or want to have? What does education represent to you?

- ♥ Where does religion and spirituality fit into your life? Do you believe in God? Do you want to share the same religion or spiritual practices with a partner? Do you envision raising children with a particular religious or spiritual orientation?

- ♥ How do you spend and save money? Do you have a lot of debt? What are you saving for (for example, material goods, travel, experiences)? What types of things do you value spending your money on? What types of purchases do you consider extravagant? At what amount of money do you start to second-guess swiping your credit card?

- ♥ What are your career goals? How demanding is your career? Do you value a work-life balance? What does a work-life balance look like to you?

♥ How do you enjoy spending your leisure time? Do you prioritize time for hobbies and passions? Is it important to you to share the majority of your interests with a partner? How much of your downtime do you want to spend with a partner? On a scale from 1 to 10 (1 = couch potato, 10 = energizer bunny), how much energy do you have to be out and about exploring, running errands, and having adventures? How much time do you want to spend with your partner when you're not working?

♥ How important is living a healthy lifestyle? Do you have strong views about diet and exercise? What are your daily self-care practices? How do you manage stress?

♥ How important are friendships in your life? How do you balance friendships when you're in a relationship?

♥ How important is sex to you? Are you traditional or adventurous in your sexual preferences? How frequently do you like to have sex when you're in a relationship? What expectations do you have about sex and a future partner?

♥ In what type of environment do you want to live? Are you a country bumpkin or a city dweller? How much does your environment contribute to your mood and general happiness? What type of home do you want to live in, and is the size of your house important to you?

♥ Where do you stand politically? Do you have conservative or liberal beliefs? Is it important to you that your political beliefs align with a partner's?

♥ Do you care about making the world a better place? Do you value giving back or volunteering with a community group or cause?

Once you get clear on your stances, think about the values your ideal partner embodies. What character traits do you value most? Is it someone driven and motivated, someone laid-back, honest, generous, open-minded, kind, charitable, or humorous? Do you prefer a risk taker, or someone who plays it safe? In order to begin thinking more critically about your partner must-haves, let's do a creative exercise.

EXERCISE: CORE VALUES VISION BOARD

For this exercise, you'll need:

- ♥ Magazines
- ♥ Poster board
- ♥ Scissors
- ♥ Glue
- ♥ Additional craft supplies such as markers, colored pencils, and you can never go wrong with glitter
- ♥ An uplifting playlist that gets you in the creative zone

We're about to go old school and create a real-life vision board instead of one on Pinterest. Something about going out to the store to buy a poster board, then sitting down with a stack of magazines and some music feels much more intentional, inspirational, and therapeutic than scrolling through trending images online.

Your core values vision board is going to embody everything that's important to you, and how you envision your life in the future with a loving partner. Based on your responses to the core values questions, collect and cut out images that best represent who you are, what you value most, the lifestyle you want to live, the qualities that describe the ideal match that you want by your side, and how you envision living life in a fulfilling, happy relationship. In twenty years from now, how do you envision your lives together? Where will you be living, what will you be doing, will you have a family, will you be on vacation, or working hard? Try to visualize what you've accomplished together, and how you want to feel about each other. Get as detailed as possible. You have full creative license here, there's no right or wrong when it comes to artistic expression!

Below are some core value questions to explore with a partner as you begin to date them. Ask the questions related to your own core values first, since these things will be the most important to you, and you'll quickly be able to identify any deal breakers. My recommendation is to explore many if not all of these questions before entering into an exclusive, committed relationship, which means typically within the first five or so dates. Though you may be dating someone casually, the conversations you have with them shouldn't be casual. You need to dig deeper. Having these conversations early on in your courtship will save you potential heartache later. They are qualifiers so that you won't get swept away by the love potion, and they will force you to honor yourself. A mature partner who's emotionally available will welcome these types of deeper discussions and not be scared away by the fact that you know who you are and what you want, whether it's kids, paying off your student loans, or that you're looking for a partner who will enjoy going to your family's Sunday night dinners.

CORE VALUE QUESTIONS FOR A PARTNER

- ♥ What do you care most about in life? What are you passionate about?

- ♥ How do you enjoy spending your leisure time? What does a typical weekend look like for you?

- ♥ Is work-life balance important to you? How do you struggle to find this balance?

- ♥ What do you do to stay active and healthy?

- ♥ What are some of your favorite things to do for self-care?

- ♥ What's your idea of adventure?

- ♥ How do you measure success in life?

- ♥ What does your ideal future look like? (Notice what they mention first, and explore all aspects of this question, including lifestyle, career, relationship/marriage, and family.)

- ♥ What do you value the most in a partner? What's most important for you to have in a relationship? What does a successful relationship look like to you?

♥ What are your deal breakers? What are the most important lessons you've learned from your past relationship experiences?

♥ What's your relationship like with your family? How do they influence how you live your life?

♥ What are your career aspirations? Do you like what you're currently doing? What aspect of your job do you enjoy the most? When you were a kid what did you want to be?

♥ What kinds of things do you like to spend your money on (travel, clothing, concerts)? What's an important lesson you learned about money growing up?

♥ Are you religious or spiritual? What holidays or traditions do you celebrate? Is it important that your partner shares or supports your religion?

♥ Do you have kids or want them in the future? When you think about raising them, what stands out as being important? What do you think the best part about having kids is/will be? What do you think the most challenging part of having kids is/will be?

♥ What are your political beliefs? What social and economic policies are most important to you?

♥ How do you give back to others? Do you volunteer? What causes are most important to you?

These questions are just examples and should open the door for ongoing conversation. If your date shares some information that might be a deal breaker, be sure to fully explore the topic with follow-up questions, and share your own views and opinions. Again, we all have beliefs that may not be identity-defining core values, so see what your date is open or flexible to changing once they learn more about your stance. However, no matter how sexy someone is, if you stumble on something you've identified as a deal breaker in your core value work, you must call it like it is and get out.

You can't expect someone to change, and there's no sense in investing time if it would ultimately require you to compromise on your own core values, whether around finances, monogamy, religion, having children, or politics. Better to find out sooner rather than later, right?

A quick note about money, since this topic often makes people anxious. It's time to get naked—financially naked! When it comes to dating, money shouldn't be a taboo topic. As a couple, you need to be financially transparent, and discuss things like your debt and money management, the same way you talk about other core values. Though you don't need to disclose your income or debt on a first date, it should absolutely come up before moving in together or getting engaged—the earlier, the better.

What you learn about each other's spending and saving habits will help you make an informed decision as to whether this person could be a compatible long-term partner. The way we spend money typically reflects what we value. In a 2015 *Money* poll, five hundred millennials rated financial responsibility just as important as a sense of humor (88 percent), and significantly more important than physical attraction (66 percent) and bedroom chemistry (58 percent). Sixty-two percent of millennials thought they'd have a stronger relationship if they combined finances before marriage. Seventy-five percent reported having a good sex life with a partner they trusted with money, compared to just 34 percent who didn't trust their partner with money. The top three reported arguments couples had over money were about overspending on frivolous purchases, not understanding the household budget, and a lack of emergency savings. Clearly finances play a big role in not only the life you want to live together, but your ability to get along and even have a fulfilling sex life, which is why you *must* talk about it during the courtship process.

Even with an ideal match, you'll still hit some bumps along the way, but because you initially aligned your core values, you'll hit smaller bumps instead of giant potholes. Consciously selecting your best match now will significantly reduce the potential conflicts you face as a couple in the future.

CHAPTER 16

Dating Questions
Answered

There are plenty of books out there about dating, whether you're looking to do it organically—like when you meet someone at Whole Foods (pun intended!)—or virtually; so this is not the time or place for a full how-to guide. However, I do have a few words of wisdom to impart as you embark on your dating journey to find lasting love. A lot of my clients feel totally overwhelmed and frustrated with the ever-changing nuances of modern dating, *especially* online dating, and I bet you do too. Quickly evolving technology has had a significant impact on the dating world, and if you don't stay up to date, you might get lost in a sea of apps, etiquette, and relevant dating terms. Here are some modern dating definitions to wrap your pretty little head around in the era of the "dating apocalypse," as *Vanity Fair* termed it:

DATING DICTIONARY

Ghosting: When someone you've been dating or talking to with the intention to meet in person drops communication and disappears abruptly, without warning or explanation.

Fadeaway: When someone you've been dating or talking to with the intention to meet in person engages in slow distancing and avoidant behaviors, such as canceling future plans, no longer calling, taking longer to respond to texts, and eventually straight-up ignoring you.

Zombieing: When someone ghosts you and then comes back from the dead to try to revive the relationship, typically with a bad excuse about what happened.

Submarining: When someone ghosts you and resurfaces down the road without an explanation or acknowledgment of what happened.

Haunting: When an ex or former fling passively creeps on your social media accounts and engages just enough for you to know he or she is there; this differs from *lurking*, which is total stealth mode.

Breadcrumbing: When someone strings you along by giving you just enough attention and minimal interest, such as a flirtatious DM on social media or a noncommittal text to lead you on, but it never goes anywhere.

Benching: When someone isn't sure if they want to continue dating you, so you're benched, put on the back burner, or added to a rotation while they search for someone better; a slow kiss of death.

Catfishing: When someone uses a fake identity online, which typically involves stealing someone else's photos or personal information, to make you fall in love with them.

Kittenfishing: When someone paints an overly positive picture of themselves online and presents themselves in an unrealistic way, such as by using outdated or overly edited photos, fibbing about their height or work title, or anything else that makes them seem better than they are in real life.

Situationship: When you're romantically involved with someone but haven't labeled the relationship formally; you're more than friends with benefits, but less than boyfriend/girlfriend status.

Textationship: When you're romantically or sexually involved with someone who primarily communicates through texts, and who doesn't put in the effort to see you in person; typically one or both partners struggle to communicate about their feelings.

Don't let these dating definitions scare you. Many were probably coined by those scorned and burnt out from swiping. Although dating apps have quickly changed the romantic landscape, there are still plenty of quality, secure singles out there looking for love, both online and IRL (the latest lingo for "in real life"). If the last time you were single was before Facebook, Snapchat, and Coffee Meets Bagel (no, that's not a Starbucks competitor), you have some adjusting to do. Never before could someone "slide into your DM's" on Instagram and ask you to meet up. Don't panic—you have time to acclimate, and my advice is to try to accept rather than reject these advances, since the online world can open many doors to connection. Online dating is no longer for nerds, desperate daters, and early adopters, so hop on the train! The reality is your ideal match could be online or offline, and *how* you meet is much less important than the fact that you now have this person in your life. Modern dating does come with its own unique challenges, however, so I'll leave you with answers to some of the most popular dating questions that I receive from my clients, on social media, and as an expert contributor for major national sites.

How can I use online dating to my advantage, what should I look out for, and what should I say?

Online dating is (ironically) a tool to help you have more real-life serendipitous dates; a way to cross paths with hundreds of people you might not otherwise meet. Your job when online dating isn't to shop profiles, carry on a conversation, and walk away with a new boyfriend. It's to decide which individuals are worth meeting for a date because chemistry must be measured in person. Same as if you chatted with a hottie on the subway, engaged in some banter, exchanged info, and decided to go out on a real date.

Sifting through online profiles can be consuming. That's why it's important to remember they're simply a taste of one's personality and values. Don't be overly critical! You might not be thrilled by his Metallica shirt in the third photo, but had you originally met in person and only discovered his love for Metallica on date four, you'd realize his many other box-ticking qualities offset his fashion choice. A highly superficial glance might prevent you from meeting a quality person.

I recommend asking yourself three basic questions: Are you attracted to this person? Do they seem to have a good personality? If they approached you at a bar, would you be intrigued or open to chatting? If yes, swipe right.

Messaging is a slightly different story. While not everyone is a gifted writer, quality banter is a good indicator of chemistry. Overall, I suggest an 80 percent rule. If, between the profile and chat, you're excited by 80 percent, agree to meet in person.

Unfortunately, no one app/site owns the market on "quality people looking for a committed relationship." They all contain the full spectrum of underlying motivations, from casual hookup to ready-to-get-down-on-one-knee. Even Tinder (yes, I'll say it!) can be a source of quality matches. The key is to identify red flags (such as overtly sexual talk or blank profiles) and keep your eyes peeled for thoughtful profiles that include comments about wanting a relationship, or imply it with couple-oriented language.

A stellar profile comes to life when you read it. Everyone can write a list of adjectives, but that doesn't make you stand out from the rest. To distinguish yourself and show you're a quality dater, follow my advice: *convey it, don't say it!* What I mean by that is paint a picture of your best qualities or interests. Instead of saying that you're funny, write something funny. Instead of writing "adventurous, traveler, foodie, animal lover" write, "Zip-lined through Costa Rican rainforests, biked my way through Napa vineyards, and swam with penguins in the Galapagos." Add in something to show you're serious about love, such as "looking for my brunch-mate and BFF who's ready to make every other couple jealous."

Don't complicate messaging strategy. Aim for a simple opener and the closer you approximate a real-life conversation the better. Imagine a guy approaching you in a bar saying: "I see from your profile you've hiked Machu Picchu. I also like hiking. I hiked the Alps last summer. What was the best part of your trip? Mine was getting to the top and appreciating the stunning views." First off, while thoughtful, it feels unnatural. Secondly, online dating is (for better or for worse) a rapid volume game; no one has time to read an essay! You don't want to scare them off with a list of questions, a giant paragraph, or some intensive thought-provoking question that's too hard to answer quickly. Instead, you could simply skip the formal salutation and say, "Hi, what's your next international vacation?" which demonstrates you're paying attention to the fact that they've traveled abroad. You might also include an additional comment about yourself such as "I just booked a week in Greece in March." Then let the conversation take its course as if you're two interested people chatting IRL naturally. Avoid sounding demanding— "Tell me what's happening in your fourth photo"—even if you're genuinely curious. And no need to tell them how much you love their profile. Don't worry. If they're active on the app, attracted to your photos, or appreciate something you wrote in your profile, they'll respond.

I advise not investing too much time messaging with someone through an app/site before going on a first date. Aim for "days" not "weeks" to meet up. If you like the banter, exchange numbers, and if you're still unsure, a quick phone screen is perfectly acceptable and something I encourage my clients to do since you can tell if there's chemistry over the phone. Your time is precious, so when a date falls flat in person, it's even more disappointing if you've invested weeks texting. All you have to say is, "Give me a call," or "I'd like to chat on the phone before meeting up in person." If they can't be bothered to call, they're not worth your time. In sum, aim to go out on a date within the first week of chatting, but remember, not everyone is checking the app/site constantly or has notifications turned on, so sometimes a few hours or even a day between messages (when you first start chatting) is acceptable. If they haven't asked you out yet, an easy nudge is to say, "So when are you going to ask me out?" with a winky emoji at the end.

So where exactly can I meet a handsome hunk in real life?
The same way that quality men (and women) are on every online site, good guys are everywhere in real life too. They aren't all hiding out in one bar, gym, or coffee shop without you. Start with pulling out your ear buds, and looking up from your phone. The opportunity for connection is all around

you, but you need to be present and confident to engage in these moments. If your goal is to meet someone, then every time you leave the house you need to make a conscious choice to be present and aware of your surroundings. The key to meeting "in the wild" begins with your nonverbal body language, and it's actually quite simple. All you need to do is lock eyes for about three steady seconds, and flash a smile. Seriously, that's the secret. Make sure to do this a few times, since it's easy to miss. One trick I like to recommend to my clients, which works like a magnet, is thinking a flirty, sexual thought when you lock eyes, such as "I know you want me," or "I know you're checking me out, and you want to come talk to me." It may feel silly, but it gives you that extra boost of confidence and may even make you crack a smile. They'll be drawn to that smile.

A man interprets a few of these eye exchanges as a green light that you're approachable and won't reject him. Since we all fear rejection, you want to send as many friendly vibes as possible. If he approaches you, all you have to do is say hello, and not get overwhelmed about the outcome of the conversation. If he hasn't approached, take some extra steps to show that you're interested by sitting or standing closer to him, whether it's in line at the grocery store or a nearby table at the café. Find a contextual reason to break the ice.

For example, if you're in the grocery store, ask the cute guy how to tell if a certain fruit is ripe; at the bar ask someone for a drink suggestion or make a joke that his big shoulders are blocking you from the bartender's view and ask him to order for you; or at the gym ask that beefcake if he knows any good stretches. If all else fails, just say hi. Laughing, giving him a compliment, or breaking the touch barrier, like touching his arm, are signs that you're into him. You can't control whether or not he's single or attracted to you, but if he is then you've just taken the steps to being asked out. And of course nothing is stopping you (but yourself) from asking for his number either.

Traditionally, men are the hunters, but if it's a matter of a missed connection I always recommend being brave and initiating contact if he hasn't. Worst case is he's not available or interested; best case is you just started a convo with your ideal match. Just make sure to give him plenty of opportunity to then take the lead so that you're not doing all of the initiating and planning yourself. I've noticed that a lot of my smart, successful, #bosslady clients live in their masculine energy at work, and then bring it into their love lives. We all embody both masculine and feminine energy, but I don't like referring to these energies with a gender reference, so we'll call masculine energy "thinker" and feminine energy "feeler." Thinker energy involves structure, planning, logic, discipline, and control, whereas feeler energy embraces emotion, intuition, receptivity, creativity, and vulnerability. When we live in our thinker energy, we feel stressed, overworked, inflexible, and unloved. When we stay only in our feeler energy, we feel irritable, overly emotional, and out of control. We need a balance, especially in our love lives. The good news is that you've already learned some great tips on how to live more in your feeler energy, such as by unpacking and working through your breakup baggage, trusting your intuition, listening to your inner voice, and taking off your armor so you can be emotionally available to new love. Receiving this love may be where you get stuck, especially if you pride yourself on being independent, self-sufficient, and a leader (thinker energy). Receiving means giving up some control, especially about the outcome of the relationship, which means being present instead of worrying about where it's heading. Sit back and allow the person you're dating to put in the effort to win your affection. You balance their efforts by being a good receiver, which means you're responsive to their efforts—such as by praising them for their choices, like the restaurant they picked for your second date, and appreciating all that they do to try to make you happy, whether it's a quick call on their lunch break to say they're thinking of you or helping you move boxes into your new apartment. When you take away the pressure of feeling like you have to always be in charge, and allow someone to pursue, you'll notice that you're less stressed and can enjoy the courting process.

To find your ideal match, think strategically about where the type of people you're attracted to hang out. If you're into the bar scene, is your ideal partner at a dive bar, a microbrewery, or a trendy lounge? If you're looking for someone with altruistic values, try a volunteer organization; if you're hoping to find a health-conscious partner, join a running club; or if you're looking for someone cultured and worldly, attend an event hosted by a local museum or a fundraising group. Just remember to add in that eye contact and a smile and flirty thought, and that might be all it takes to form a connection.

Your goal is to create as many windows of opportunity as possible to meet and mingle with new people. Ask your friends to tap into their extended networks and introduce you. Accept invitations to parties, BBQs, and happy hours. Go out with coworkers after work. Unless you're online dating, you're not going to meet anyone at home, so break out of your typical routine. One of my clients really wanted to date a medical doctor, so she'd eat lunch at the hospital café next to her office building and practice making eye contact with all the McDreamys and McSteamys in scrubs.

Check out other location suggestions below, and in all cases, think about the towns and type of facility to increase your chances of meeting someone of your desired socioeconomic status:

- ♥ Workout classes (yes, men do go to yoga, but try other types of fitness facilities, such as an MMA gym, rock climbing, or CrossFit)
- ♥ Bookstore, library, or book club
- ♥ Professional networking events
- ♥ After-work events that bring together multiple departments
- ♥ Comedy club (either as an attendee or sign up for an improv class)
- ♥ Local festivals in your community, including farmers' markets, concerts, and art shows
- ♥ Coffee shops and restaurants, especially special tastings and events
- ♥ Home Depot
- ♥ Brewery or wine tasting venue
- ♥ Intramural sports leagues
- ♥ Adult education classes
- ♥ Public park or dog park
- ♥ Common areas at universities or in the lobby of a corporate office building
- ♥ Places of worship

What should we do on a first date, who should pay, and should we seal it with a kiss?

Think of a first date as a meet-and-greet to figure out if there's enough physical attraction and common interests to warrant a second date. The best topics to kick off with are the hobbies and interests that you're most passionate about, which should tie into your core values. The only off-topic limit should be your ex, since only 14 percent of singles in the *Singles in America* survey by Match.com said they were up for chatting about this. If your date asks, or you feel inclined to bring up your ex, the appropriate way to do so is by talking about your personal growth experiences, such as your love lessons and what you now realize you need and are looking for in a partner or desire in a relationship (without ex-bashing).

Aim for a casual and low pressure first date, without a ton of time and money invested. It's easier to commit to something with a distinct start and end, where you don't have to stick around longer than you want to if there's no chemistry. Start with a drink, which can always be extended into apps or a meal if you're having fun; otherwise, you have an easy excuse to wrap up when you get to the bottom of your glass. If you drink alcohol, skip the beer and wine and go straight for a cocktail, which was found in Match's *Singles in America* survey to increase your second-date chances by 137 percent! Don't sweat it if you don't drink, though; you can still make a plan around coffee, tea, or ice cream. If you feel confident that you'll hit it off because of your prior conversation, then sitting down for a real dinner date may feel appropriate. In this case, your best option is to go out for sushi. Seriously! The survey found that a sushi date increases your chances of having a second date by 170 percent. I can attest to this, since my first date with my husband was over sushi. But the survey also found that two and a half hours gives you the best odds of scoring a second date; nothing more, nothing less. We had a five hour marathon first date (sushi>drinks>basketball), so perhaps it's best to treat these as guidelines but not rules. Rules are strict and inflexible, and your love story is a unique journey.

Another topic that comes up often is who's responsible for paying the bill at the end of the date. Gender norms and roles are changing in our society, which will ultimately affect dating norms. From an evolutionary perspective, women value men who can provide resources because it ensures that their young will survive. In modern times, this looks like socioeconomic status, ambitiousness, intelligence, owning property, and having a good job. Now that women have their own money, property, and good jobs, should dating etiquette change to reflect societal changes? That's for you to decide. You may be a successful, independent woman and still welcome being cared for in this way, or you may want a more equal playing field. Ultimately, if you embrace more progressive values and feel strongly about going Dutch, this will make for a valuable conversation with your date, since your reasoning likely reflects your core values. See how they respond and whether your beliefs and values align. Just keep in mind that although it's only a first date, you're searching for a dependable and reliable partner, and little generous gestures like picking up the check, or at least the intention to pay (91 percent of women want their date to insist on paying on a first date, according to the 2018 survey results), speak volumes about how you'll be treated in the future. Be flexible in how you approach bill paying so that you can adapt to the situation. For example, if one person said they'd like to take you out to dinner or treat you to an experience, it's likely they will foot the bill. However, if you're chatting online and one person casually suggests that you meet up for coffee or hang out, this situation is more ambiguous and, at minimum, expect to split. The financial standing of each person should be taken into account too. For example, if you're a poor student dating another poor student, it might be the most financially responsible choice to split the bill; or if one person makes significantly more money than the other, allow them to pick up the tab. Interestingly, the 2016 *Singles in America* survey found that 50 percent of men and 36 percent of women agree that a man should pay on the first date, which means half of the men and two-thirds of the women disagree. However, the 2017 survey results show that of the women who do split, almost nine out of ten do it to feel free of any postdate hookup obligation. What's your stance?

To kiss or not to kiss is another key question. Half of the men and women in the Match.com survey think (only) kissing is appropriate on a good first date, while 44 percent say that a kiss is inappropriate no matter what the circumstances and prefer to wait. What's difficult to determine is what constitutes a "good" first date, since oftentimes attraction and chemistry are in the eye of the beholder. What we know does not make good impressions are some first-date faux pas, such as checking your phone, being more than fifteen minutes late, and having more than two drinks. Signs that your date is feeling you is if they are making consistent eye contact and smiling a lot, are offering compliments, and have broken the touch barrier or at least made efforts to sit or stand very close to you. A handshake goodbye is likely a sign that they're just not that into you, whereas a long hug with your bodies pressed together and lingering eye contact sends the message you both want to end the date with a smooch. Don't fret if you wanted a kiss and didn't get one; they may be traditional and fall under the 50 percent who don't think kissing on a first date is appropriate.

What about *more* than kissing? Let's say sparks are flying and the chemistry is hot. You've had your first PG-13 kiss, and now you're questioning if you should make it an R-rated kind of night. The survey results suggest you better hold off on anything more intimate, since only 15 percent of men and 7 percent of women expect a "make-out session" on a first date, and only 6 percent of men and 1 percent of women expect to have sex. If you're both into each other, then what's the rush? Sometimes a slower build can be even more erotic and enticing. Plus, leading with your sexuality can come off as though you're compensating for low self worth, and after all the hard work you've put into loving yourself, you need to set the boundary that you respect and value yourself, so that they will too. Your goal is to be put in the girlfriend bucket, not the hookup bucket, and there are other flirty ways you can show them you're interested without taking off your pants.

Oh, and if you're wondering how to manage social media when you're first seeing someone, here's how singles stack up according to the 2018 survey results: 41 percent add someone on social media after they've been out a few times, 19 percent add before the first date, 18 percent add once things get serious, and 15 percent add after a good first date. There are pros and cons to allowing someone to see your social media accounts before getting to know them. What do you want them to know about your life? Be aware people make quick judgments and assumptions based on your photos and what you post. You also have to deal with defriending them if it doesn't work out, so I recommend at least waiting until you've been out multiple times and know you like them and want to give them more access to you.

GENERATIONAL ATTITUDES

A quick note about millennials, the generation most familiar with dating apps, having sex early on, and delaying marriage. What's worth noting here is that the recent data from the 2017 *Singles in America* survey found that millennials are 48 percent more likely than other generations to have had sex *before* the first date. What we're seeing is sex occurring earlier on as a qualifier to figure out if the person you're interested in is worth a commitment. Twenty-eight percent of the millennials surveyed said they view sex as a way to decide if they love someone or not. Although millennials may be rushing into the bedroom, they're certainly not sprinting to the altar. Pew research studies tell us that young adults today attach less moral stigma to living together before marriage, so many couples cohabitate, sometimes for years, before taking their relationship to the next level. This generation is more approving of having children out of wedlock too, so they may feel less motivated to make it official before having a baby together. Millennials are under a lot of pressure to establish their careers and pay off enormous student loans, which may delay moving out of mom and dad's place to save money; so they could also be hesitant to enter into a serious relationship without being in the privacy of their own house rather than their parents' home.

These factors contribute to the delay of marriage, as well as to the seismic shift in belief that modern marriage is now more about personal fulfillment. Millennials have said goodbye to the days of saying "I do" solely for the purpose of procreating, child-rearing, and purchasing a home. This mental shift means they're more focused on "Does my partner make me happy?" and "How does my partner improve my life?" Settling has become a major turn-off; rather, millennials are searching for their soul mates. They're holding out for someone truly special who meets all of their needs—physically, emotionally, spiritually, environmentally, politically, and financially. As a millennial myself, I love Dr. Helen Fisher's optimistic prediction that we may see a decreased divorce rate with this generation. Since millennials are living together longer before marriage, this allows them time to test out the relationship and work through conflict before determining whether they want to be with their partner for the rest of their lives. Naturally, some of these relationships will dissolve, but they don't have to deal with the legality of marriage and divorce. Those who do choose to marry will have tested their relationship before getting hitched, so hopefully we'll see a trend of longer, happier marriages; they'll just start later in life than past generations. Marriage used to be the beginning of a relationship, but now Fisher says it's the finale!

How do I let someone down without hurting their feelings?
Is ghosting ever okay?
I get it; you feel anxious at the thought of letting someone know you're no longer interested, and you're wondering if ignoring the situation or subtly decreasing communication would be easier for both parties. However, if you're emotionally mature enough to date, you should be emotionally mature enough to have a breakup convo. Psychologically, it's more confusing and hurtful to ignore someone because they're left in the dark about what went wrong, and as you know, we tend to blame ourselves and think we're not good enough. This dilemma has spawned the phenomenon of *ghosting*, which, as discussed in chapter 5, is when you disappear out of someone's life without a word or explanation. The right way to end a relationship is not to leave the person you're seeing wondering if you've died. Changing your Facebook status to single is certainly not the way your partner deserves to find out it's over. Why would you treat someone in a way that you wouldn't want to be treated? If ghosting was the way in which your big breakup ended, then I'm sure I don't have to convince you that it's not the right way to end things. If you're emotionally mature enough to date, you should be emotionally mature enough for a breakup convo.

Ghosting is a selfish act and viewed as an easy solution to avoid broaching a difficult, emotionally wrenching conversation. We do it because it makes us feel less awkward and uncomfortable—it's really not about taking the other person's feelings into account at all. One of the reasons people increasingly don't think twice about ghosting is because of our reliance on technology, which to some extent dehumanizes us into little emojis on a screen. The benefit of social media and online dating apps has been *huge* in the dating world. All of this technology allows us to interact with new people daily, and it's made meeting, dating, and hooking up so much easier; but at the same time, it's damaged our communication skills. For instance, when we don't make eye contact or read facial expressions, it's very difficult to know how our words and behaviors impact someone else. When you communicate through a screen, you can say whatever you want to someone, or completely ignore them, without having to physically face the consequences of seeing their heart break, or hearing their voice crack and eyes well up when you tell them it's over. We lose these important forms of feedback on how we've impacted someone else when we communicate through text, or disappear instead of delivering difficult news.

Ghosting has damaging consequences on our mental health, such as increasing anxiety and self-doubt, and it ties up our emotional resources. The last thing we need is another scorned, bitter, and cynical person back on the dating market. Being straightforward saves this person mental anguish and time spent overanalyzing your noncommunicative behavior. Here are some assertive ways you can kindly and clearly let someone down:

♥ It was great meeting you, but I didn't feel any chemistry.

♥ I had a blast but I got more of a friend vibe.

♥ It's been nice chatting, but I don't think we're a match.

♥ You seem wonderful, but I don't feel a spark between us.

♥ I don't see this going in the direction of a serious relationship and that's what I'm looking for at this time in my life.

♥ Thanks for making the time to get together; I wish there was something more between us, but I don't feel a romantic connection.

♥ You're a catch, but unfortunately just not my catch.

♥ I like you, but I don't think we have enough shared values to make this work in the long run, so it needs to end here.

Sometimes it can be confusing as to when you owe someone a letdown response and when you don't. Good thing I'm here to break down some general ghosting etiquette:

♥ If you received a message online, you're under no pressure or obligation to respond if you're not interested.

♥ If you've been corresponding with someone who expressed interest in getting offline (either asking for your number or asking to meet in person), a simple comment such as "It's been nice chatting with you, but I don't see this going any further" is sufficient. If they persist and ask why, it's your choice whether you want to respond.

♥ If you're only in the getting-to-know-you phase, such as after a first date, it's okay to go your separate ways in silence if no one expressed interest in a second date. However, if one person asks the other for another date, you must directly communicate your desire to cut things off.

♥ If you've been out on about five or more dates, there's a relationship budding and you probably exchanged some emotionally intimate conversations. At this point you owe your partner a face-to-face conversation, or at least a phone call to tell them what's on your mind.

No one has a magic mind-reading power, so courteous dating behavior is about letting someone know your intentions—to move forward, or end it. Sometimes there can be an innocent misunderstanding when one person feels a connection and the other has no interest in pursuing it any further. But, expecting them to take a hint from your silence is rude. If you're not feeling it, it's important to be transparent and straightforward. Someone with a secure attachment doesn't play games. Let's take a stand against ghosting. In the words of the famous *Ghostbusters* song, "If there's something weird and it don't look good, who you gonna call . . . ?" The answer should be your partner, so that you can break things off the right way!

I've had so many bad relationships. How do I know that I'm being treated right, and how should I feel?

First, you set the standards for how you want to be treated. After my friend Natasha went through a tumultuous breakup, she decided she wasn't going

Rule #1
Never be anyone's
number two.

@LOVESUCCESSFULLY

to settle again for a boyfriend that didn't prioritize her and meet her needs. When she started dating a busy entrepreneur, she wasn't happy about the fact that he didn't reach out to talk to her one day in their early dating history. Instead of being passive aggressive about it or playing games, she simply told him during their next conversation that if he wants to date her, her expectation is that they will communicate daily, and she wants to hear his voice, not just texting. They've talked every day since. Your standards should reflect the way that you ideally want to be treated in a healthy, secure relationship. Are you honoring your relational needs and core values and showing up authentically as a version of you that you admire in this budding relationship? If not, you're probably repeating negative patterns and operating from an activated attachment style. Be more upfront and vulnerable about what you want from your new partner, and actually ask for it!

Once you've examined your own behaviors and conclude that you're open, assertive, and receptive, you can turn your attention toward them. If a quality, secure partner is interested in you, then there are certain common behaviors that they'll engage in over the first few months of courting you. If you can't check off these simple boxes, then they're likely not treating you the way that you deserve. Assertively address the issue once, but if they're unresponsive, peace out. Your self-esteem and self-worth are high, so you're not sticking around!

- ❑ They followed up after a date to let me know they had a good time.

- ❑ They make plans in advance for a next date.

- ❑ They put in effort to do fun things, instead of Netflix and chill.

- ❑ They send a message or call just to say hi, with the frequency of communication increasing the longer we're together.

- ❑ They give me thoughtful compliments.

- ❑ They treat me with kindness and respect.

❏ They're physically affectionate, and move at a pace that I'm comfortable with for sexual intimacy.

❏ They open up and talk to me about substantial topics, such as family, friends, work, and life goals, and welcome core value conversations.

❏ They're generally a positive person, and even when they have a bad day at work they don't take it out on me.

❏ They consistently put in effort and invest emotionally after we started having sex.

❏ They're responsive to my physical and emotional needs.

❏ I feel safe, secure, and that I can trust them.

❏ I feel desirable and appreciated.

❏ I feel like a priority.

❏ I feel comfortable being my authentic, true self around them, and that I'm not pretending to be someone else for praise and validation.

❏ I'm focused on getting to know them and evaluating whether I like them, and not as concerned about whether they like me.

❏ I'm giving equally to the relationship, and not putting in all of the effort; I'm investing as much as they're investing in me.

❏ I'm not compromising on any of my core values in this relationship.

❏ I continue to invest in my individual goals and friendships, and have created a balance where my world does not revolve around them.

❑ We're able to talk through conflict in a calm way without criticizing, demeaning, swearing, or yelling.

❑ We continue to progress, grow, and bond as a couple after every date.

If you've noticed the following red flags, get out *now*!

❑ They're rude to our waiters or other strangers we interact with on our dates.

❑ They don't respect my boundaries, like when I tell them I need to be home by a certain time or that I need a night to myself.

❑ They're possessive or jealous.

❑ They constantly check in and need to know what I'm doing or who I'm with.

❑ They only want to hang out late at night in private (booty call).

❑ They pressure me to have sex or do things I'm not comfortable doing, and they may try to normalize this experience by telling me what other women they've been with have done.

❑ They lose their temper easily, and their anger is disproportionate to the trigger that set them off.

❑ They're judgmental and critical of my appearance.

❑ They expect me to be exclusive, while they date multiple people.

❑ They lack control over alcohol or drugs and aren't getting help.

You'll know you're dating from a secure attachment style when:

- ♥ Dating is an enjoyable process, and you're not filled with dread or anxiety.
- ♥ You believe that you're a catch and that there are many great options for you out there.
- ♥ You believe you have the power to pick a good partner, rather than settle for someone.
- ♥ You're straightforward with your new partner about developing feelings.
- ♥ You don't spend a lot of time worrying if they feel the same way about you, and you're not afraid to have an exclusivity conversation.
- ♥ If someone isn't treating you the way you want, you move on.

If you have an anxious attachment style, you can shift to a more secure base with the following tips:

- ♥ Be aware that intense highs and lows signal an activated attachment style, and don't misattribute this roller coaster to being in love.
- ♥ Acknowledge that healthy love is safe, trusting, reliable, consistent, and dependable.
- ♥ Don't confuse easy with boring or a lack of connection.
- ♥ Remind yourself that secure love can be slower to develop or feel less of a challenge because you're used to dating someone avoidant. So be patient, and fireworks may develop.
- ♥ Remind yourself that in secure love, you won't be left in the dark, wondering what page you're on.
- ♥ Think of someone in your life who has a secure attachment

or healthy relationship and ask yourself how they would handle conflict or a situation that makes you feel on edge.

If you have an avoidant attachment style, you can shift to a more secure base with the following tips:

- ♥ Notice when you start to push someone away or search for things not to like about them, and instead make a list of what you admire about them.

- ♥ Remind yourself that although you are very capable of being self-sufficient or that you don't need someone's opinion to make a decision, part of creating a healthy relationship is having a teammate mentality and sense of interdependence.

- ♥ Acknowledge that relying and depending on a partner doesn't make you weak.

- ♥ Ask yourself, "What would a good teammate do in this situation?"

- ♥ Rather than run away, attempt to get comfortable with intimacy, even if it feels overwhelming at first.

- ♥ Think of someone in your life who has a secure attachment style or healthy relationship, and ask yourself how they would handle conflict or a situation that makes you want to distance yourself.

Why does it seem like everyone is hesitant to commit, especially with online dating?
You think things are going well—maybe you've been out on two or three dates—but out of boredom or curiosity, you log into your dating app, and that's when you notice that the person you've been seeing is signed on too. You think, *What are they looking for? Aren't I enough?* You feel slightly annoyed, confused, and upset all at the same time, but then you realize you're also doing the exact same thing.

One aspect that could be affecting commitment is the fact that swiping apps are simply addicting. To some extent, dating apps are treated like a smartphone game where profiles are no longer regarded as real people with feelings, but rather as points to win a game and boost your self-esteem. It's like Candy Crush, but instead of brightly colored candy, you're swiping on people's faces and hoping for a reward by matching or receiving a message. Apps like Tinder and Bumble activate the reward center of the brain, where each connection releases a burst of dopamine that makes you feel excited. You become trained to swipe over and over again, seeking that "high" every time you match. Since many of these apps have recently limited the amount of swipes you can have in a certain period of time, this leaves you craving more, unless you pay to upgrade—umm, how do you think Candy Crush became a billion-dollar company? Because you never know who will swipe right, it's enticing to keep going. You match just enough when you log in that you're intrigued or even obsessed with coming back to the app. It's not surprising that the 2017 *Singles in America* survey found that 22 percent of millennials feel technology has made finding love more difficult, millennials are 57 percent more likely to have created a profile on a dating app than any other generation, 127 percent more likely to admit they're addicted to the process of making a love connection, and 57 percent of millennial respondents reported being lonely.

With the ease of online apps and sites, it's basically like 24–7 shopping for a date or relationship. There's hundreds of potential partners available at the swipe of your finger. I call this dating FOMO the *grass is greener* mentality. Everyone seems to want the next best thing, and it's killing dating mojo. When we expect instant results, we're less likely to go on a second or third date if we don't see the entire relationship play out before our eyes, so we look elsewhere. People are hesitant to put in more effort and enter into a committed, exclusive relationship because within two seconds of swiping right, you could meet someone "better." The problem with this is that you could miss out on your ideal match sitting right in front of you. I think dating multiple people early on is a great strategy so that you don't have all of your eggs in one basket, but once you meet a potential keeper, you need to dive in vulnerably knowing you could get hurt.

This grass-is-greener, commitment-phobe mentality may be due to choice overload, which is when you have difficulty making a decision because you're presented with too many options. It's like having analysis paralysis, so rather than make a commitment you keep looking at other possibilities because you're afraid of making the wrong choice. Findings in the *Journal of Consumer Research* show that an excess of choices often leads us to feeling *less* satisfied once we actually make a decision, which you may experience when you agree to become exclusive and slightly panic that you're making a mistake. However, this typically goes away with time once you become more familiar with each other and start building memories together. Notice, I just said it takes time to build connection. Because you're dating with intent, you know what you want and need, so the next step is testing it out when you've found someone with potential. If they make you feel loved and happy, stop shopping and try it out.

To minimize the overwhelm, I tell my clients they're only allowed to be actively messaging and dating five people at a time. If they want to match with someone new, they must rule someone out to create space. This also causes them to be more intentional with who they're swiping on and forces them to either initiate a convo or unmatch. When you have fewer options to pick from, you'll invest more time into getting to know someone. Some dating apps, like The League and Coffee Meets Bagel, are catching on and giving you a limited number of hand-curated matches so that you can focus on quality rather than quantity.

We aren't a resume or a checklist, we're humans. It takes time, communication, and digging deeper to evaluate someone who may have potential. Relationships are built on this effort and intimacy, and when you're half in and half out you're not nurturing the relationship to grow. At some point you need to put both feet in—or should I say both *fingers* in, stop swiping, and commit to giving it a real shot.

Here's the deal: breaking up is always an option. Now that you're experienced in surviving and moving on from heartbreak, the worst-case scenario shouldn't be a relationship ending, but rather passing up an ideal match because you were afraid to put energy into getting to know them when the outcome wasn't guaranteed. It's time to commit when after every date you feel that you're getting to know this person better and can't wait to learn even more. When not only is there physical chemistry, but your core values and life visions are aligning. There's always new, attractive, and interesting people to meet in life, but at some point you have to ask yourself whether you want a relationship and if you're happy with the person you're casually seeing. When that answer is yes, an exclusive commitment is the only way to see if this budding relationship can be a forever love.

I'm ready for a commitment, but I'm not sure they are.
How do I tell?

You're ready to proudly change your status from single to being in a relationship, but you're unsure where your partner stands. Are you just one of many in their hookup rotation, or do they seem committed to moving forward with only you? If you have an anxious or avoidant attachment style, this may be a particularly confusing stage in a relationship. Mixed signals and feeling in the dark should ring an alarm bell that you may not be with a secure partner. No matter your type, the start to a relationship can be rocky, isn't always black and white, and feelings can develop at different paces. But, there should be clear signs that it's progressing forward. If you're tuned into their behavior, you should be able to recognize that a partner with a secure attachment will communicate their feelings for you, tell you that they like you, and ask you to be exclusive. They might even tell you that they deleted their online profile. Their actions match up with their words, and all signs point to the fact that they're smitten with you. Since relationships go two ways, you should also be giving verbal and behavioral signs (being receptive, appreciative, and complimentary) that you're into them too and happy to be progressing forward. I'm sure by now you know what I'm going to say—this requires vulnerability, especially if you're the first to show your cards, such as telling them that you like them and have been enjoying their company.

When it's not so straightforward, it's likely because they're saying one thing and doing another. This is the telltale sign of an emotionally unavailable partner. If they're telling you how much they like you or miss you, but they're not actually planning dates with you or prioritizing time with you, they're not invested, and this is yet another game that you no longer have time to play since you upped your standards. For example, if they miss you, why don't they pick up the phone and call you or plan a date to see you, instead of sending a lazy text? Or, if you're so amazing, why are they only ever able to take you out on a Tuesday night, but conveniently busy on the weekends? It can be confusing, like when you have an incredible date where you thought you took the relationship to the next level, but then they don't call you for a week. Stop riding the wave of the push and pull. They can feed you smooth lines that roll off of their tongue, but words lack meaning when behaviors don't back them up.

Here's a quiz to help you figure out if they're ready for a real commitment. Remember, relationships only work when both partners are emotionally invested.

1. They're going through a divorce, very recently single, or their Facebook status says, "It's complicated."
 Yes ❏ No

2. They make plans with you a week or even a month in advance. ❏ Yes ❏ No

3. They swipe on Tinder and message women in front of you. ❏ Yes ❏ No

4. They introduce you to their friends and are eager to meet yours. ❏ Yes ❏ No

5. They blow off your plans or don't accommodate your schedule. ❏ Yes ❏ No

6. They find ways to make you feel special or prioritize you even when life gets busy with work and other obligations.
 Yes ❏ No

7. They're secretive with their phone or social media accounts. ❏ Yes ❏ No

8. They share their vulnerabilities, fears, and insecurities with you. ❏ Yes ❏ No

9. They keep conversations surface level.

❑ Yes ❑ No

10. They use "we" instead of "me" when talking about plans or the future. ❑ Yes ❑ No

11. They have not introduced you to their network.

❑ Yes ❑ No

12. They woo you with meaningful dates, compliments, or small gifts based on information they've learned about you.

❑ Yes ❑ No

13. They use sex to gain intimacy, instead of intimacy to gain sex. ❑ Yes ❑ No

14. They're trustworthy, reliable, and make you feel safe.

❑ Yes ❑ No

15. They don't talk about the future with you.

❑ Yes ❑ No

16. They're open to trying your favorite hobbies and exploring your interests. ❑ Yes ❑ No

17. They make you feel insecure about where the relationship is headed, or their affection is inconsistent.

❑ Yes ❑ No

SCORING

♥ Give yourself +1 point for every "yes" answer

♥ Add up your total score for the even-numbered questions =

- ♥ Add up your total score for the odd-numbered questions =
- ♥ Subtract the odd total score from your even total score (even total – odd total = Final Score)
- ♥ My score = ???

RESULTS

- ♥ 8 = GOOD GUY: They're a keeper and the relationship is heading in the right direction.
- ♥ 4 = Look out for red flags and remember actions speak louder than words.
- ♥ 0 = You deserve better; own your worth, woman!
- ♥ −4 = They're just not that into you and they're playing hard to get.
- ♥ −9 = BAD BOY: They want their cake and you're letting them eat it too.

Someone who said all of the right things may have duped you in the past, but it's time to stop making excuses for inconsistent behavior. I'm not big on inflexible dating rules, but in this case, rule number one is to never be anyone's number two.

Sometimes men like to try you on for size. What I mean by that is they like to imagine what it would be like to date you and have a future with you, so they get excited and start saying everything you want to hear, creating a false sense of security very early on without an actual commitment. It's like taking a car out for a test drive, but when it comes to buying the car, he doesn't pull the trigger. Basically, in his mind, you're a sexy Lamborghini, but you deserve to be more than just a fun joyride.

A secure, emotionally available partner who's ready for a commitment will show you through their behaviors that they're into you, especially when you reciprocate their affections. They'll court you, woo you, and move mountains to win you over. There'll be a sense of safety and security in your relationship, and you won't have to waste your time wondering how they're feeling because you'll already know.

When should I have a "define the relationship" (DTR) talk and what should I say?

With online sites and dating apps there's so many nuances with modern-day dating. There's chatting online, which moves to text or phone calls, then to casual dating (which can last a few dates or months), which develops into exclusive dating, and then a defined BF/GF status. Are you exhausted just thinking about it? Today's singles want to define each stage of the relationship and desire transparency about where they stand, which is a positive shift since that requires you to date from a secure base. Because everyone has a different approach, it can be confusing which stage you're in unless you talk about it directly. That's why it's important to have a DTR ("define the relationship") talk to make sure you're on the same page.

Timing for the DTR talk is unique to each couple because it depends on what each partner is looking for and whether having an official title is important to them. Some people will throw it right out there that they only date one person at a time; others will tell you they're casually dating multiple people and need to get to know you better before making a commitment; and of course there are those who have a secret rotation of dates and hookups. The only rule is to *never assume exclusivity, even (heck, especially!) when you're sexually active.*

Forming a relationship takes vulnerability, knowing you could be met with rejection when you express your feelings. Don't let the fear of rejection hold you back, since this vulnerability is the birthplace of love. If it's reciprocated and you're both equally invested, it creates a rewarding sense of security that allows each partner to open up, be more expressive, and develop an even stronger bond where you continue to grow together. To get to this point, one person has to be brave and show their cards first in order to move forward. Hiding under your armor for too long can stunt the growth of the relationship. I know it can be nerve-wracking, but to progress you need to be able to talk about and process your relationship and emotions with them.

When my husband first asked me to be his girlfriend, I actually turned him down since I wanted to be extremely intentional about the next person I committed my heart to. I told him that despite not being ready for a girlfriend title, I saw long-term potential and shared with him the qualities I liked in him, and how we could be a strong match. He understood that I needed to move a little slower, so he patiently waited as we continued to check in with each other along the way about how our feelings were progressing. I assured him that if I determined he wasn't the man for me, that I wouldn't waste his time. He continued confidently in his courtship. Being able to talk to him openly about vulnerable and uncomfortable things, like the status of my feelings for him, and knowing he was a clear communicator, put me at ease. Over the first few months into dating, we chatted about our core values, and saw that we had similar life goals. I realized none of our differences overlapped with my deal breakers, and that in general I loved being around him. You know how the rest of my story ends. If you find yourself in a similar situation, the fact that you, as a collective couple, can communicate openly about where you are at emotionally in the early stages of dating is a great sign that you'll be strong communicators in the future relationship.

In your new narrative for love, one in which you embrace your needs and desires, and feel worthy, you should no longer tolerate being kept at a distance. If you've been waiting awhile for them to bring up a DTR talk, you can initiate a productive conversation with the following lead-ins:

- ♥ How do you think our relationship is going?
- ♥ I'm having a lot of fun spending time with you and I just wanted to tell you that I really like you. I'm wondering, how are you feeling?
- ♥ How do you feel about us only seeing each other?
- ♥ Just so you know, I deleted my profile; how do you feel about doing the same?

Notice these questions are open-ended, so they are meant to be conversation *starters*. Carefully listen to their entire response and give them a chance to elaborate. For example, if they say, "I really like you, but I'm just not sure what I want right now," they're not telling you they want a commitment. Well, what do they want? If they stumble over their words or you're unclear about their response you can follow up with, "How do you see us moving forward?" If your partner says they're enjoying getting to know you but needs more time together before making a commitment, it's your choice whether you want to be patient and stick it out. If that's not enough for you, your response can be, "I really like you, but I can't continue to invest emotionally if we're not on the same page."

You deserve a partner who's willing and open to creating a committed relationship. If they're not ready at this moment to date you exclusively, they should at least be able to tell you how they feel about you and provide a path for moving forward. You need to be prepared to walk away if you don't get the answer you're hoping for, or one that honors your needs. Stop playing the chill girl, waiting around forever in hopes that they realize you're girlfriend material. I've worked with too many women who were clinging on for dear life, only to feel disrespected, unappreciated, resentful, and taken advantage of later on when they never got the commitment they chased after.

A partner who wants a relationship with you will welcome an exclusivity convo and give you a clear response. Someone who dodges the conversation or gives you some vague answer isn't interested or has an avoidant attachment style and struggles with these types of discussions around intimacy. A man who tells you that he's not looking for a relationship right now actually means it, so stop overanalyzing. When someone tells you who they are, believe them! Bottom line, a partner who wants a relationship will be enthusiastic about the idea of building a future with you. Then a few actions should come after a DTR talk. Both partners need to delete their online dating profiles. Calls or messages should be sent to the other people you were dating to let them know that you're officially off the market and will no longer be able to see them. Once you've made it to this stage and the relationship is official, here's how you might declare it on social media (according to the 2018 *Singles in America* survey): 66 percent of couples make it Facebook official, 66 percent change their profile picture to a couple's pic, 65 percent friend their partner's family, and 52 percent friend each other's friends.

How do I know if they're my ideal match?
You've had discussions about the lifestyle you want to live and what matters most to each of you. You've waited for the love potion to wear off, the honeymoon phase is over, and you've successfully dealt with conflict. You've made peace with the annoying things that you can't change about them, and have confidently determined you're not compromising on any deal breakers. You experience happiness most days with your partner and are filled with

gratitude that they're in your life. Your heart and head are in alignment; you've created a simpatico relationship. When you've found your keeper, you should be able to check off the following relationship statements:

❑ **We pass the sweatpants test.**

Do you have just as much fun being silly in sweatpants together on the couch as when it gets hot and heavy in the bedroom? The intense, passionate, all-consuming love in the early honeymoon stage should develop over time into a deep, committed, companionate love. Of course there's still passion and desire, which in the long term takes effort to maintain, but there's a deepening friendship as well. Many relationships fizzle out during this transition once your brain chemistry calms down, and some enter into that status "quople" zone. When your blinders come down and you see this person more fully, do you still love what you see? You may realize that your connection was more about the physical relationship and the intimacy underneath was stunted. You can feel safe thinking about marriage or a lifelong partnership when you continue to grow and connect.

❑ **Life is better with them by my side.**

If you agree with this statement, then you much prefer the company of your partner than anyone else when going through your day-to-day activities. No, I don't necessarily mean you'd rather get a mani-pedi with him than your best gal pal (though kudos to the men who enjoy that), but when they're not there, you miss their presence or can't wait to catch them up on what they missed. It's more than the obsession of being apart when you're newly in love, or jealousy and insecurity that comes with an anxious attachment; rather, it's that you genuinely enjoy living life with this person next to you every day. When you become best friends with your partner, it takes your connection to a whole new level, with deep emotional intimacy. You can talk about anything, and you foster an underlying respect for each other. When you're with your ideal match, you undoubtedly have the "we factor" over the "me factor." For example, when you talk about weekend plans, you instantly take each other into consideration, thinking, "What are *we* going to do?" instead of "What am *I* going to do?" You function as a unified team, and check in with your partner when making decisions.

❏ **I feel like the best version of myself in this relationship.**

In this relationship, do your behaviors and actions align with who you want to be and the life you want to live? Do they bring out the best in you? Have you hopped off the roller coaster and feel calm, secure, and safe? With the right partner, you'll feel like the best version of yourself, whether that's more kind, driven, motivated, creative, patient, or peaceful. Your family and friends likely give you positive feedback and make statements such as "You seem really happy together." You feel you can be your authentic self, and they see and accept all of you. Red flags are if you often feel jealous, insecure, needy, depressed, crazy, angry, or anxious in the relationship, in which case you should go back and reread the core concepts in this book!

❏ **I don't want to change a lot about them.**

There are no perfect people or perfect relationships. Rather than get swept away by romantic love, which is based on passion and sexual attraction, it's important to balance this with pragmatic love, which are the practical aspects of how your lives align based on things like your desired lifestyles, personality traits, and core values. Be intentional about choosing your partner by utilizing my ideal match theory so that you can figure out if there are any deal breakers before you commit to life together. Recognize that if you choose to accept your partner as is, you actually have to let go of the expectation that they'll change in the future. At this point it's best to focus on what you love, rather than on what's lacking. If you're struggling to overlook the things you don't like, remember that the practice of gratitude can be an extremely powerful tool in helping you let go of the things that get under your skin. Gratitude research shows that if you feel and express gratitude for your partner today, you'll feel more connected and satisfied in the relationship tomorrow, and that couples who expressed gratitude for each other not only had a more positive perception of their partners but also felt more comfortable voicing concerns about their relationship. When in doubt, be with the person you want to change the least, and choose to focus on what you love about them.

❏ **When I think of my future, it includes them.**

I know this statement sounds simple, but after all of the clarity you've gained from your heartbreak, you now have the skill set to pick a better match for yourself. You're no longer making this decision just because you're in love, you have great sex, or you're afraid to call it quits after investing time, energy, and finances into the relationship. You've owned your worth and found someone who truly values, cherishes, and respects you. You're picking this person because they're your ideal match, and it's resoundingly clear—a no-brainer—that you can see a clear future together. On the contrary, when reading this statement, if you were filled with dread or anxiety at the thought of spending your happily-ever-after with them, then that's your inner voice telling you something. Listen to it! If you find yourself constantly wondering if you could do better, or your physical and/or emotional needs are not being met, it may be time for a breakup conversation, which you're now very prepared to handle, survive, and bounce back from.

CONCLUSION

Wow. Can you believe how far you have come? You've already started living that fabulous postbreakup life I mentioned at the beginning of this book. You can finally see that you dodged a bullet. Hallelujah! You survived zombie mode, and have nourished your body with self-care and proper diet, sleep, and exercise. You courageously rode the grief roller coaster from denial through bargaining/anxiety, anger, and depression; turned upside down a few times and even backwards, but finally exited safely on the sturdy ground of acceptance. Rejection is one of the most difficult human experiences, and you learned to cope like a champ. You practiced mindfulness and learned anxiety management tools, such as a dwell spell, gratitude journal, and deep breathing meditations to ease your obsessive thinking. You created an ex-free environment and challenged your automatic negative thoughts. You learned about the neuroscience of a breakup, which shows that love is a positive addiction that you withdraw from when you split up, which explains your body's physiological response and cravings for your ex. You gained understanding about the reasons for your breakup, including differing attachment styles, love languages, and conflicting core values. You identified cracks in the relationship that led you to realize they were definitely not your ideal match. You've embraced the idea that relationships are not black and white, so you no longer define the relationship with your ex by the fact that it ended, or how long it lasted, but rather by what you learned about yourself throughout the experience.

Looking to the future, you'll never stuff down that little inner voice again and will trust your own intuition. One of the most important outcomes of your breakup is your ability to invest in yourself and start owning your worth and honoring your needs. You created a new sense of purpose in your social, personal, and professional life that fills you up. You committed to practicing self-love, and today, in this moment, you can affirm that you are enough and accept yourself as you currently are. You're no longer willing to settle or compromise on your values, and you want more out of a relationship than to be a complacent status "quople." You have learned that just because you put in a lot of time, effort, love, and finances into a relationship, it doesn't mean you should continue to invest if they're not the right person. You turned inwards to reflect on your love lessons, took responsibility for any wrongdoing, and wrote a healing letter of self-forgiveness. You identified emotional injuries from childhood that caused you to make negative assumptions about yourself and love. You've decided to let go of your old framework and create a new secure adult narrative for love—one based on feelings of worthiness, a mind-set of hope and abundance, and the ability to show up vulnerably and authentically in your dating life.

You've gained motivation to find your ideal match, and you're cognizant of getting carried away by the love potion of neurochemicals that influence your mood. You're aware of the importance of aligning core values, complementary personalities, and a shared life vision to create a secure, stable, successful long-term relationship. You're committed to being a smarter, more intentional dater, and approaching your love life with confidence, even in the face of rejection. Ideally, only one relationship will work out in the long run, so you've accepted that breaking up is part of the weeding-out process. To move more intentionally through your dating life, you're committed to strategically collecting and analyzing dating data along the way, allowing it to inform your dating decisions and enabling you to choose an ideal match. When searching for your best match, you'll honor what you label as deal breakers, and accept what you can't change. You'll remain open to receiving the love you deserve, and will love your future partner wholeheartedly and fiercely, the same way you love yourself.

I'm so grateful that you took this healing journey with me and have found a new purpose in life. You're incredibly strong, brave, courageous, and worthy of love. Let's say it one last time together, and then I'll leave you here, knowing you're able to stand on your own two feet, with the support of friends and family, and motivated to step up and create the love life you desire:

"Today I choose to lower my defenses, to love myself, and to see myself as worthy. I choose to show up vulnerably so that I can attract and receive the love that I deserve."

BIBLIOGRAPHY

Ansari, Aziz, and Eric Klinenberg. *Modern Romance*. New York: Penguin Books, 2016.

"Attachment Style and Rejection Sensitivity: The Mediating Effect of Self-Esteem and Worry among Iranian College Students," https://ejop.psychopen.eu/article/view/463

Bernstein, G. (2017, October 9). *How to Release the Story Victim*. Retrieved from GabbyBernstein.com: https://gabbybernstein.com/release-story-victim/?inf_contact_key=68e424c64e9ed2a3a72fab3c81167b391bf323d-faaaddb6b2cf20a9b609e441b

BMJ-British Medical Journal. (2011, January 28). Marriage is good for physical and mental health, study finds. *ScienceDaily*. Retrieved October 26, 2017 from www.sciencedaily.com/releases/2011/01/110127205853.htm

Brown, PhD, LMSW, Brené. *Daring Greatly*. New York: Avery Publishing, 2015.

Brown, PhD, LMSW, Brené. *The Gifts of Imperfection*. Center City, Minnesota: Hazelden Publishing, 2010.

Chapman, Gary. *The Five Love Languages*. London: Strand Publishing, 2000.

Davis, Laurie. *Love @ First Click*. New York: Atria Books, 2013.

Festinger, L., Schachter, S., & Bach, K. (1950). "Social pressures in informal groups." New York: Harper.

Fisher, PhD, Helen. *Anatomy of Love.* New York: Ballantine Books, 1994.

Fisher, PhD, Helen. *Why Him? Why Her?* New York: Henry Holt and Co., 2009.

Gomez, S. L., Hurley, S., Canchola, A. J., Keegan, T. H. M., Cheng, I., Murphy, J. D., Clarke, C. A., Glaser, S. L. and Martínez, M. E. (2016), Effects of marital status and economic resources on survival after cancer: A population-based study. Cancer, 122: 1618–1625. doi:10.1002/cncr.29885

Harlow, H., Dodsworth, R., & Harlow, M. (1965, April 28). Total Isolation in Monkeys. *Psychology, 54*, pp. 90-97.

http://bigthink.com/videos/helen-fisher-on-how-to-sustain-a-long-term-relationship

http://blog.pof.com/2016/03/pof-survey-reveals-80-millennials-ghosted

http://drrobertepstein.com/downloads/Epstein-HOW_SCIENCE_CAN_HELP_YOU_FALL_IN_LOVE-Sci_Am_Mind-JanFeb2010.pdf?lbi-sphpreq=1

http://journals.plos.org/plosone/article?id=10.1371/journal.pone.0161087

http://journals.sagepub.com/doi/abs/10.1177/0146167209352250h

http://journals.sagepub.com/doi/abs/10.1177/0146167215612743

http://journals.sagepub.com/doi/abs/10.1177/0265407512453009

http://journals.sagepub.com/doi/pdf/10.1177/0146167217726988

http://journals.sagepub.com/doi/pdf/10.1177/0146167297234003

http://neuro.hms.harvard.edu/harvard-mahoney-neuroscience-institute/brain-newsletter/and-brain-series/love-and-brain

http://onlinelibrary.wiley.com/doi/10.1002/ejsp.1842/full

http://onlinelibrary.wiley.com/doi/10.1111/j.1475-6811.2006.00120.x/epd-f?referrer_access_token=cnAZiAIXpZbrQeMPVPvxcYta6bR2k8jH0Krd-pFOxC67UHBVhY2Ccem-bc_BxlyIySsq8pepulw9sBgctaDhdWkriSbqu_T65G8Y-CZ2WfASTDUl3VFJfxoz_ZqAaFj2nJO-4lU4b50nRsqiG-g-2z1qT-CI8e6_5JeLNsdsjcg2UZaqJkyQBWddz4RmtRD7gwkOMIBJlo47cmS6ICEW-FYIjHBQ6vRA1jwoL3xNvlKbcK6SZ1YeyOTCfpAE5OC6SiWvaVfmvMLJ-wj4GFQaQbLVX9gMXvYD27B6SAkQ9Q3og45mEpqts-Gj7hqJo7ZpyRXL

http://onlinelibrary.wiley.com/wol1/doi/10.1111/pere.12173/abstract

http://psycnet.apa.org/record/1991-12476-001

http://psycnet.apa.org/record/1992-38948-001

http://time.com/money/3882484/couples-money-survey-boomers-millennials

http://www.dailymail.co.uk/femail/article-2573879/Youre-breaking-TEXT-Dont-worry-youre-not-one-digitally-dumped-splits-happen-SMS.html

http://www.npr.org/templates/story/story.php?storyId=128795325

http://www.nytimes.com/2010/02/27/your-money/27shortcuts.html

http://www.pewresearch.org/fact-tank/2017/02/13/5-facts-about-love-and-marriage

http://www.sciencedirect.com/science/article/pii/S0191886909004711

http://www.singlesinamerica.com/2016

http://www.singlesinamerica.com/2017

http://www.tandfonline.com/doi/abs/10.1080/10503307.2016.1169332?scroll=top&needAccess=true&journalCode=tpsr20

http://www.tandfonline.com/doi/abs/10.1080/15298868.2015.1095794

https://bmcpublichealth.biomedcentral.com/articles/10.1186/1471-2458-13-773

https://boris.unibe.ch/95490/7/Luciano%20and%20Orth%202017%20JPSP.pdf

https://gillab.ku.edu/sites/gillab.drupal.ku.edu/files/docs/GBSWM05.pdf

https://greatergood.berkeley.edu/article/item/love_gratitude_oxytocin

https://greatergood.berkeley.edu/images/application_uploads/Algoe-GratitudeAndRomance.pdf

https://theanatomyoflove.com/the-results/ventral-tegmental-area

https://www.gottman.com/blog/the-magic-relationship-ratio-according-science

https://www.psychologytoday.com/blog/open-gently/201310/36-questions-bring-you-closer-together

https://www.ncbi.nlm.nih.gov/pmc/articles/PMC2753321

https://www.ncbi.nlm.nih.gov/pubmed/19073292

https://www.ncbi.nlm.nih.gov/pubmed/21401225

https://www.ncbi.nlm.nih.gov/pubmed/26514295

https://www.ncbi.nlm.nih.gov/pubmed/?term=Grewen+K+2003

https://www.nytimes.com/2015/01/11/fashion/modern-love-to-fall-in-love-with-anyone-do-this.html

https://www.psychologytoday.com/blog/close-encounters/201702/the-5-most-important-qualities-romantic-partner

https://www.psychologytoday.com/blog/insight-therapy/201412/laws-attraction-how-do-we-select-life-partner

https://www.psychologytoday.com/blog/open-gently/201310/36-questions-bring-you-closer-together

https://www.psychologytoday.com/blog/the-mindful-self-express/201104/the-neuroscience-relationship-breakups

https://www.theatlantic.com/health/archive/2016/01/romantic-rejection-and-the-self-deprecation-trap/424842

https://www.webmd.com/sex/features/sex-drive-how-do-men-women-compare#1

Johnson, Dr. Sue. *Hold Me Tight*. New York: Little, Brown and Company, 2008.

Kübler-Ross, E. (n.d.). *The 5 Stages of Grief*. Retrieved October 2017, from Grief.com: https://grief.com/the-five-stages-of-grief

Larson, G., & Sbarra, D. (2015). Participating in Research on Romantic Breakups Promotes Emotional Recovery via Changes in Self-Concept Clarity. *Social Psychological and Personality Science*, *6* (4), 399 - 406. https://doi.org/10.1177/1948550614563085

LeVeque, Kelly. *Body Love*. New York: William Morrow, 2017.

Levine, MD, Amir, and Rachel S. F. Heller, MA. *Attached*. New York: TarcherPerigree, 2012.

Lewis, MD, Thomas, Fari Amini, MD, and Richard Lannon, MD. *A General Theory of Love*. New York: Random House, 2000.

Lindquist, K. (2016, September 9). *Does labeling your feelings help regulate them?* Retrieved from Emotion News: http://emotionnews.org/does-labeling-your-feelings-help-regulate-them/

Page, Ken. *Deeper Dating*. Boulder, Colorado: Shambala Publishing, 2014.

Parker-Pope, T. (n.d.). *How to Have a Better Relationship*. Retrieved from New York Times: https://www.nytimes.com/guides/well-how-to-have-a-better-relationship?action=click&contentCollection=famly&contentPlacement=1&em_pos=small&emc=edit_hh_20171011&-module=package&nl=well&nl_art=0&nlid=44142507&pgtype=section-front&redirect=true&ref=headline&region=rank&rref=collection%2Fsec-tioncollection%2Fwell-family&te=1&version=highlights

Pedre, MD, Vincent. *Happy Gut*. New York: William Morrow Paperbacks: 2017.

Robak, Boyan and Griffin, Paul, "Dealing With Romantic Break-Up and Rejection: Understanding the Nature of Relationships and Romantic Break-Up" (2012). *Student–Faculty Research Projects*. Paper 4. http://digital-commons.pace.edu/ugfacprojects/4

Schwartz, Barry. *The Paradox of Choice*. New York: Ecco Press, 2016.

Sigal, J. J., Perry, J. C., Rossignol, M., & Ouimet, M. C. (2003). Unwanted infants: Psychological and physical consequences of inadequate orphanage care 50 years later. *American Journal of Orthopsychiatry, 73*(1), 3-12.

Sincero, Jen. *You Are a Badass*. Philadelphia: Running Press Adult, 2013.

Tatkin, PsyD, MFT, Stan. *Wired for Dating*. Oakland, California: New Harbinger Publications, 2016.

Tatkin, PsyD, MFT, Stan. *Wired for Love*. Oakland, California: New Harbinger Publications, 2012.

Thomas, Katherine Woodward. *Conscious Uncoupling*. New York: Harmony Books, 2015.

Wolpert, S. (2007, June). *Putting Feelings Into Words Produces Therapeutic Effects in the Brain; UCLA Neuroimaging Study Supports Ancient Buddhist Teachings*. Retrieved from UCLA Newsroom: http://newsroom.ucla.edu/releases/Putting-Feelings-Into-Words-Produces-8047

BOOKS TO ADD TO YOUR COLLECTION

Anatomy of Love by Helen Fisher, PhD

Attached by Amir Levine, MD and Rachel S. F. Heller, MA

Body Love by Kelly LeVeque

Conscious Uncoupling by Katherine Woodward Thomas

Daring Greatly by Brené Brown, PhD, LMSW

Deeper Dating by Ken Page

The Five Love Languages by Gary Chapman

The Gifts of Imperfection by Brené Brown, PhD, LMSW

Hold Me Tight by Dr. Sue Johnson

Love @ First Click by Laurie Davis

Modern Romance by Aziz Ansari and Eric Klinenberg

Why Him? Why Her? by Helen Fisher, PhD

Wired for Dating by Stan Tatkin, PsyD, MFT

Wired for Love by Stan Tatkin, PsyD, MFT

You Are a Badass by Jen Sincero

ABOUT THE AUTHOR

Samantha Burns, LMHC is "the Millenial Love Expert," combining the clinical background of a therapist with the voice of a best friend. She runs a private practice in Boston and consults with clients around the world, partners with Match.com as a dating expert, and has been featured in *Women's Health*, *Brides*, *Huffington Post*, *Reader's Digest*, *Cosmopolitan*, and *Elite Daily*.

Women as
Mythmakers

The Ideal Life (La vie idéale), Léonor Fini, 1950, oil, 36-1/8″
× 25-5/8″.
Courtesy of Léonor Fini.

Women as Mythmakers

Poetry and Visual Art by Twentieth-Century Women

Estella Lauter

INDIANA UNIVERSITY PRESS

Bloomington

To My Family
Judson and Edna Loomis
Chuck, Kristin, and Nicholas Lauter
and to the members of our extended family

Library of Congress Cataloging in Publication Data

Lauter, Estella, 1940–
　Women as mythmakers.

　Bibliography: p.
　Includes index.
　　1. Feminism and the arts.　2. Women artists.
　　3. Art and mythology.　I. Title.
NX180.FL38　　1984　　700'.88042　　83-48636
ISBN 0-253-36606-2
ISBN 0-253-20325-2 (pbk.)
1 2 3 4 5 88 87 86 85 84

CONTENTS

Preface vii
Acknowledgments xiii

INTRODUCTION: Steps toward a Feminist Archetypal
Theory of Mythmaking I

Part One: Individual Visions

CHAPTER 1 Anne Sexton's Radical Discontent 23
CHAPTER 2 Käthe Kollwitz: The Power of the Mother
(with Dominique Rozenberg) 47
CHAPTER 3 Margaret Atwood: Remythologizing Circe 62
CHAPTER 4 Remedios Varo:
The Creative Woman and the Female Quest 79
CHAPTER 5 Diane Wakoski:
Disentangling the Woman from the Moon 98
CHAPTER 6 Léonor Fini:
Re-envisioning La Belle Dame sans Merci 114

Part Two: Collective Visions

CHAPTER 7 Mythic Patterns in Contemporary Visual Art by Women 131
CHAPTER 8 "Woman and Nature" Revisited in Poetry by Women 172
CONCLUSION The Light Is in Us 203

Notes 225
Bibliography 247
Index 261

Illustrations

Frontispiece	Léonor Fini	*The Ideal Life*	
Plate 1	Käthe Kollwitz	*Seed Corn Must Not Be Ground*	51
Plate 2	Käthe Kollwitz	*Tower of Mothers*	54
Plate 3	Käthe Kollwitz	*Death with a Woman*	60
Plate 4	Remedios Varo	*Solar Music*	82
Plate 5	Remedios Varo	*The Creation of the Birds*	85
Plate 6	Remedios Varo	*Still-Life Being Resurrected*	87
Plate 7	Remedios Varo	*Born Again*	93
Plate 8	Léonor Fini	*The Sending*	124
Plate 9	Léonor Fini	*Capital Punishment*	125
Plate 10	Léonor Fini	*The Strangers*	126
Plate 11	Ellen Lanyon	*Bewitched Teacup*	136
Plate 12	Mary Frank	*River Figure*	145
Plate 13	Patricia Johanson	*Estuary/Maze House*—Plan	148
Plate 14	Nancy Graves	*Hurricane Camille*	161
Plate 15	June Wayne	*Visa*	168

PREFACE

These essays on women poets and visual artists, on myth and feminist criticism, have taken their present shape over a period of six years; but the question that inspired them first emerged more than ten years ago when I taught my first courses in women's studies and myth studies as part of the developing interdisciplinary curriculum at the University of Wisconsin–Green Bay. I wondered: would contemporary poetry by women provide an illuminating case study of mythological change? In the past, I reasoned, new myths arose in times of profound cultural crisis such as our own. Perhaps one of the most important changes of this century has been the phenomenon of population explosion, which, in countries where medical technology has also prolonged the human lifespan, has meant that women have no longer needed to concern themselves primarily with the survival of the species through procreation. For the first time in history, large numbers of women have been free to pursue activities of their own choosing outside the home. Such a profound change in the human situation would seem likely to affect our cultural mythology, and the most logical place to look for such effects would be in creative works by women. My question presupposed that myths change in relationship to history; that creative individuals play a role in changing them; and, most important, that myths are still significant phenomena in our lives. Thus one question, about the difference women poets might make in our cultural mythology, became many: Why are myths significant? How are they related to history? How do they interact with individual lives? *How* do they change? How *much* do they change? These and other questions were addressed in dozens of books which I began to read along with the poems by women that occupied the center of my attention. Of course, I know now that many critics and many books will be required to answer my initial query, and I offer this book as a probe into the question rather than a definitive study.

For four years, I read without writing more than notes for lectures and symposia, and then I began to focus on individuals: on Margaret Atwood because she had deliberately remythologized a well-known figure from Greek mythology; on Anne Sexton because she had struggled so valiantly with the Christian myth; on Diane Wakoski because she had worked her way through the troublesome mythic equation of woman with nature. But this account makes my choices seem more rational than such choices ever are; I might as well say that Atwood's Circe chose me to interpret her according to the same inner logic that caused me to write my own poem about Circe. (Ultimately, it is that inner logic whereby we, as artists or as critics, identify with one figure, revise another and discard a third that I would like to understand.) Certainly, my choices were also guided by my knowledge that these poets evoked strong responses from contemporary audiences; but I might have chosen many others on the same grounds. My process of choice was as inductive as possible. That is, I read hundreds of poems with nothing more in mind than open-ended questions such as these: Does the poet directly or indirectly engage a figure, symbol, or narrative from traditional mythology? If so, why does she do this? How consciously does she enter into a process of revision? What attitude does she ask us to assume toward myth? Does she create alternative images, figures or stories that might some day have the status of myth if they were embraced by others?

In 1976, I gained access to a large slide collection of visual works by women and began to show them to my classes. I was amazed both by the images and by the responses they evoked, and I began to think how they, too, might be linked to myth. As I explored those works of art with students and colleagues, it seemed to me that the descriptions of archetypes I had learned from the Jungian tradition were being altered before my eyes, and other images were being formulated, of the same apparent status but hitherto undescribed. I wondered if these images belonged to either ancient or modern stories that, like Circe's, had not yet been told. My questions about the relationship of image to story led to others about the nature of archetype and myth. Do Käthe Kollwitz's images of the mother in her later work evoke such strong responses because they belong to the ancient lore of the mother goddess, or because they awaken in us an untold story about who or what we might be in the future (or both)? Do Remedios Varo's multiple paintings about the female quest actually create a story (instead of reflecting on parts of a narrative that was already known)? Does her vision of a distinctively female quest mean that archetypes are gendered? And what about the paintings of a female society by Léonor Fini? Are they examples of an even more radical process of mythmaking? Are images less bound by convention than words, so that visual artists are more free to envision our lives in mythic terms than are poets? Was this the case in ancient times as well?

All these questions were formulated by the time I participated in a National Endowment for the Humanities Summer Seminar on "Myth, Symbolic Modes, and Ideology" in the summer of 1978. Between 1976 and 1981, I presented early drafts of several chapters at meetings of the Modern Language Association, the National Women's Studies Association, the American Academy of Religion, and conferences featuring the work of C. G. Jung. Versions of four essays were published in interdisciplinary journals, reflecting my epistemological commitment to an interdisciplinary process of validation. In 1980, I organized a Special Session at the Modern Language Association, engaging three poet-critics, Alicia Ostriker, Sandra Gilbert, and Rachel Blau DuPlessis, to explore the role of myth in their own work. Also in 1980, I embarked on a new phase of my study.

Having traced various processes of mythmaking in the works of individuals in two art forms, I wanted to see whether similar activity on the part of many artists was producing anything we could conceivably call a myth. During a sabbatical year, I not only reviewed all the materials I had read and seen before but also surveyed the work of more than a thousand visual artists across the United States, using slide collections, archives, and galleries in nine major art centers in addition to resources provided by various individuals and collectives outside those centers. In this phase of my study, I looked for any pattern of image or story without regard to its connection with a recognizable myth. The most pervasive pattern I found in that body of visual art by women of many ages, colors, backgrounds, and persuasions was a network of related images concerning the process of transformation by which one form becomes another. No identifiable myth emerged from this body of work seen by itself. (It is not the primary function of visual art to tell stories, although it has done so before, usually to carry an already formed cultural mythology.) What did emerge, however, is a "new" vision of relationships among orders of being.

My search through contemporary poetry by women revealed a more extensive pattern of concerns with nature than I had seen before. Nonetheless, I had nearly decided that it did not yield a story—when it occurred to me that I might have been defining the idea of story too narrowly, too much in terms of other mythologies. Having denied in a public lecture that any text was serving the mythic function that *The Waste Land* served early in the century, I decided to test that assertion by investigating the relationship between Susan Griffin's *Woman and Nature* (1978) and the images of nature in poetry by other women. Indeed, from the vantage point of this relationship, a new myth may be taking shape. In it, nature remains female but becomes *equal* to the human.

It is, to be sure, an incipient myth whose full scope and force will be revealed only by history. I want to uncover it, and any other myths that may be in process, because I know that myths can play a powerful role in shaping human lives. But their power can be ours only if we establish viable relationships with them. Thus, although I celebrate the achievements of the individual poets and artists I present here and describe with enthusiasm the collective vision I find in the works I have surveyed, I do not offer these materials as models to be imitated. These women have not discovered truths that are outside history; they have simply responded to the imperatives of their own history in ways that may disclose the imperatives of ours.

As I will argue in my introductory chapter, when we uncover a myth or an archetype, we do not necessarily reveal a "given" of human nature. This statement may seem strange to those who recognize the influence of Jungian thought on my methodology. Certainly I have learned from Jung to look across the boundaries of cultures and artistic media for repeated images, stories, and forms that reveal the preoccupations of an era. I am even willing to call those repetitions manifestations of archetypes. But I do not see the archetype as an unchanging entity outside the process of human development. Instead, I believe it is a tendency to form an image in response to recurrent experiences. The value of the archetypal or mythic image is that it leads us back to experiential nodes that have been important for long enough or to enough people to call for response. Just as it was an important step in male psychology to locate the Oedipus complex, so it will be important to female psychology to locate similar nexuses. But contrary to both Freudian and Jungian theory, these are not un-changing realities. They are experiential parameters in a network of relationships that has both the stability and the unpredictability of human history. We expose them to establish a conscious rela-tionship with them. If my study helps to expose some of these nodes, I will be pleased.

My primary goals, however, are to explore the multiple pro-cesses of mythmaking in current use by women, and to discern the direction toward which those processes are tending. Follow-ing the introduction to the multiple issues of the book (myth and mythmaking, archetypal theory, and feminist criticism), the reader will find in Part One separate chapters on individual poets and artists, which may be read separately or consecutively, as s/he chooses. Each of these chapters addresses a different issue with a methodology drawn from the work under scrutiny. I hope the reader will feel free to adapt any of these modes of interpretation to other works, or to apply them to questions I have not addressed. Whereas the chapters in Part One deal with the entire century and with European and Mexican as well as American artists, Part Two seeks to assess the collective vision that emerged in the 1970s in the United States. I look forward to other assessments of mythmaking in different circumstances. If my findings are borne out in other contexts, women may indeed be making profound changes in our cultural mythology.

ACKNOWLEDGMENTS

This book is the result of a great deal of collaboration. Dominique Rozenberg, a native of France and co-author of chapter 2, was a graduate student in my class, Images of Women in Contemporary Arts, in January 1978, and her paper on the gestures that characterize Kollwitz's protagonists became the basis for our interpretation of Kollwitz's image of the mother. I am also indebted to Hugo Martinez-Serros, of Lawrence University, whose translation of Roger Caillois's essay on Remedios Varo was itself a work of art, and to Sharon Fenlon, from Appleton, who spent several winter afternoons with me in 1978 translating French criticism of Léonor Fini's paintings. In addition, my colleagues Kenneth Fleurant, Raquel Kersten and Martha Wallach, and my student Miriam Early from the University of Wisconsin–Green Bay have also offered their linguistic assistance at crucial moments.

Without the stimulation of my colleagues in a thoroughly interdisciplinary seminar called "Myth, Symbolic Modes, and Ideology," sponsored by the National Endowment for the Humanities at the Claremont Graduate School in 1978, I might never have envisioned these essays as a book. And without a sabbatical award from the Faculty Development Council at the University of Wisconsin–Green Bay, I certainly would never have been able to complete the research for the two thematic chapters on visual art and poetry. The Research Council, Chancellor Edward Weidner, and Communication and the Arts have also contributed travel funds to support the project. For my early training in research, I am indebted to the University of Rochester.

Many galleries, artists' collectives, and artists' registries allowed me to use their facilities and resources from 1978 to 1981; their names appear in the notes to chapter 7, but it would be impossible to enumerate the individual artists and administrators whose generosity enabled my research at every turn.

I also wish to thank the many friends and colleagues who provided material sustenance during my research trips in 1978 and 1980–81, particularly Karen Petersen at Sonoma State College; Tom and Caroline Griffith in New York; Hilde Hein in Boston; Chuck and Pat Werhane in Chicago; Don Brunnquell and Sally Scogin in Minneapolis; Bill Baer and Nancy Hendry, and Karen Laub-Novak in Washington, D.C.

Since the project began, many colleagues have provided invaluable commentary, encouragement, or editorial assistance. These include Sandra Gilbert and Susan Gubar, Diana George, Judith McCombs, Annis Pratt and Kathryn Rabuzzi, who invited me to make presentations on panels they organized for the Modern Language Association, the National Women's Studies Association, and the American Academy of Religion; and Tom Ogletree and James Hillman who were ideal editors of my early publications. In addition, Doris Grieser Marquit, Stephanie Demetrakopoulos, Ellin Sarot, Sidney Bremer and June Wayne have made insightful comments on portions of the manuscript.

Along the way, there have been wonderful conversations with Alicia Ostriker, Rachel Blau DuPlessis, Susan Friedman, Jane Tompkins, Diane Wakoski, Lisel Mueller, Marge Piercy, Camille Billops, Ellen Lanyon, and, more recently, Walter Gruen. These have helped to keep my spirits high—as have my contacts with the fellows of the Society for Values in Higher Education—at moments when the project seemed too big to complete.

This all-too-partial list of credits must also include the staff of the Lawrence University Library, particularly Harriet Tippett, Kathy Isaacson and Doris Giese, whose skill and patience have greatly extended the range and depth of my studies. Likewise the editors of Indiana University Press, particularly Susan Fernandez and Mary Jane Gormley, deserve plaudits for their expert and sensitive handling of the project from start to finish. Marie Garot has worked tirelessly on the endless typing tasks associated with the project. Jerry Dell has assisted in the preparation of photographs for the printer.

To the members of my extended family of relatives and friends who have shared important experiences with me in the past twenty years, I offer thanks for your support in the form of a book that expresses my belief in the less visible communal aspects of our lives—the ones that keep us linked even when we see each other infrequently. And to the members of my immediate family, I am grateful for your continuing affection, even under the relentless pressure of my professional deadlines.

Permissions

Four chapters of this book are based on previously published essays, and grateful acknowledgment is made to the journals for permission to reprint them:

"Anne Sexton's 'Radical Discontent with the Awful Order of Things'," *Spring: An Annual of Archetypal Psychology and Jungian Thought* (Irving, Texas: Spring Publications, 1979), pp.77–92.

With Dominique Rozenberg, "The Transformation of the Mother in the Work of Käthe Kollwitz," *Anima* V, 2 (Spring 1979), pp. 83–98.

"The Creative Woman and the Female Quest: The Paintings of Remedios Varo," *Soundings: An Interdisciplinary Journal* LXIII, 2 (Summer 1980), pp. 113–134.

"Léonor Fini: Preparing to Meet the Strangers of the New World," *Woman's Art Journal* I, 1 (Spring/Summer 1980), pp. 44–49.

Grateful acknowledgment is made to the publishers and agents for permission to quote excerpts from the following works:

Susan Astor, "The Farmer Lost a Child" and "Sea People" from Paul Feroe, ed., *Silent Voices*. Copyright 1978 Ally Press, St. Paul, Minn.

Margaret Atwood, "Notes from Various Pasts," from *The Animals in that Country*. Copyright 1968 by Oxford University Press (Canadian Branch). Reprinted by permission of Little, Brown, and Company in association with the Atlantic Monthly Press, and Oxford University Press. "April, Radio, Planting, Easter" and "A Red Shirt" from *Two-Headed Poems*. Copyright 1978 by Oxford University Press (Canadian Branch). Reprinted by permission of Simon and Schuster and Phoebe Larmore. "Book of Ancestors," "Circe/Mud Poems," "Corpse Song," and "Is/Not" from *You Are Happy*. Copyright 1974 by Margaret Atwood. Reprinted by permission of Harper and Row, Publishers, Inc. and Phoebe Larmore.

Besmilr Brigham, "Mountains" from *Heaved from the Earth*. Copyright 1971 by Besmilr Brigham. Reprinted by permission of Besmilr Brigham.

Diane di Prima from *Loba*. Copyright 1978 by Diane di Prima. Reprinted by permission of Wingbow Press.

Susan Griffin, "This Earth" and "Matter" from *Woman and Nature: The Roaring inside Her*. Copyright 1978 by Susan Griffin. Reprinted by permission of Harper and Row, Publishers, Inc., Carol Murray and Susan Griffin.

Denise Levertov, "Come into Animal Presence" from *The Jacob's Ladder*.

above reprinted by permission of Doubleday & Company, Inc. Excerpts
from *The Magellanic Clouds*. Copyright 1970 by Diane Wakoski. Excerpts
from *Smudging*. Copyright 1972 by Diane Wakoski. Excerpts from *Dancing on
the Grave of a Son of a Bitch*. Copyright 1973 by Diane Wakoski. Excerpts
from *Waiting for the King of Spain*. Copyright 1976 by Diane Wakoski. Excerpts from the last four books reprinted by permission of Black Sparrow
Press. Excerpts from *The Motorcycle Betrayal Poems*. Copyright 1971 by Diane
Wakoski and reprinted by her permission.
Nancy Willard, "When There Were Trees" from *Carpenter of the Sun*. Copyright
by Nancy Willard and reprinted by her permission.